D0618228

Country Keepsakes

Cross Stitcher Magazine's

Country Keepsakes

50 Delightful Cross Stitch Designs

future
BOOKS

First published in 1994 by
Future Books
A division of Future Publishing Limited
30 Monmouth Street, Bath BA1 2BW

Text Copyright © Future Publishing 1994
Photographs © Jonathan Fisher 1994

Individual designers are acknowledged on page 5

Designed by Paula Mabe
Illustrations by Kate Davis
Photography by Jonathan Fisher

All rights reserved. No part of this publication may be reproduced, stored in a retrieval system, or
transmitted in any form or by any means, electronic, mechanical, or otherwise, without the prior
written permission of the copyright holder.

A catalogue record of this book is available from The British Library

Isbn: 1 85981 015 2

Printed and bound in Malaysia by Times Offset (M) Sdn. Bhd.

We take great care to ensure that what we print is accurate, but we cannot
accept liability for any mistakes or misprints.

The Publishers are grateful to the following designers who have given permission for their designs to be included in this book.

Country Comforts pp 18-25:
Pauline Cartland

The Cat's Whiskers pp 26-9:
Brenda Greenslade

Down a Country Lane pp 30-7:
'Counting Sheep' Ralph Eagle; 'Squirrel' June Bridges; 'Harvest Mouse' Wendy Moore; 'Badger' Yoke Lunn; 'Hedgehog' Jaquelene Mills; 'Sheep in a Field' Charlotte Strong

Down to a Fine Art pp 38-41:
Zoe Smith

Country Nightlife pp 42-9:
'Big Owl' Julie Cook; 'Lucky Black Cat' Mrs F France; 'Owl in Moon' Kerry Allen; 'Black and Grey Cat' Mrs Collis Smith; 'Black and White Cat' Janet Skerritt; 'Red Owl' Mrs H Rogers; 'Branch Owl' Anne Easton

Summer in the Meadow pp 50-7:
Jane Greenoff
The Inglestone Collection
Yells Yard
Cirencester Road
Fairford, Glos
GL7 4BS

Wish You Were Here pp 58-61:
Brenda Greenslade

How's That pp 62-5:
Brenda Burnett

The Bear Essentials pp 66-73:
'Teddy Love Sampler' Gail Bussi; 'Teddy Bridesmaid' Jen Harris; 'Grandma's Bear' Karen Bendelow; 'Panda Bear' Naomi Jones; 'Teddy Heart' Ann Methvan; 'Teddy in Hammock' Marion Biddle

Homeward Bound pp 74-81:
'Home Sampler' Sue Cook; 'Castle' Pauline Wilcox; 'Farmhouse' Joan Hughes; 'Home Sweet Home' Hilary Goudge; 'Tree House' Patricia Bull; 'Windmill' K W Matthews

Junior Gymkhana pp 82-5:
Gillian Bowater

The Land of Childhood Dreams pp 86-93:
'Balloon Bears' Julie Cook; 'Tooth Fairy' Barbara Dawson; 'Baby Girl/Boy' Yvonne Mathieson; 'Zoo Animals' Penelope Randall; 'Bear and Butterflies' Janet Stedman; 'Joker' Joanne Kyte; 'Bottles' Tracy Medway

Perfect Timing pp 94-101:
'Clock on Mantelpiece' Sue Cook; 'Tempus Fugit' Sue Cook; 'Family Clock' Tracy Medway; 'Wake Up' Linda Blakey

Sending in the Clowns pp 102-5:
Gillian Bowater

Plain Sailing pp 106-113:
'Lighthouse' Zoe smith; 'Tall Ship and Viking Ship' Marion Biddle; 'Sailing Boat' Anna Greenwood; 'Blackwork Boat' Sally Wilson; 'Little Sea Friends' Marguitta Herzer

Earth Laughs in Flowers pp 114-7:
Gail Bussi

The Flowering of Passions pp 118-126:
'Beadwork Flowers' Gillian Leeper; 'Lavender Bag' Jane Alford; 'Les Fleurs' Tracy Medway; 'Bookmarks' Lynda Whittle; 'Tiger Lily' Jean Muir

Contents

Country Comforts

Down to a Fine Art

Country Nightlife

How's That

e Bear Essentials

The Land of Childhood Dreams

end in the Clowns

The Flowering of Passions

Stitching Guidelines and Techniques

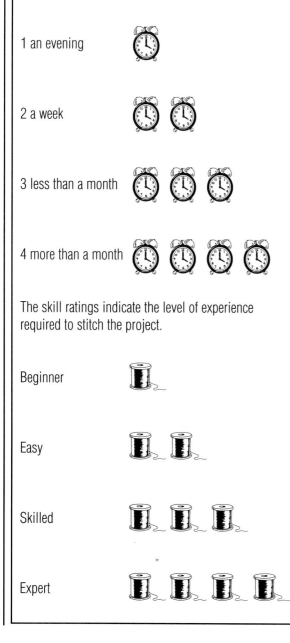

Ratings

At the beginning of each project you will find two sets of icons. The alarm clocks indicate the approximate time it would take an average stitcher of the suggested skill level to complete the project.

1 an evening

2 a week

3 less than a month

4 more than a month

The skill ratings indicate the level of experience required to stitch the project.

Beginner

Easy

Skilled

Expert

❀Materials ❀

Fabric

*F*or the projects in this book, we always advise on the type, mesh size and colour of canvas to use. You will find this information in the key to each chart. The price of canvas varies depending on its quality and is most often made of cotton, though some synthetic blended canvas threads are also available and are generally cheaper. Always buy the best canvas you can afford as you want your finished work to last a long time, but take care with some canvases as the thread may be irregular in thickness and this will show in your stitching

Once you have chosen the type and count of your canvas you should buy enough so that there will be at least two inches (five centimetres) all the way round the finished stitched area for blocking, framing and mounting purposes.

Threads

*I*t is possible to use different types of thread for cross stitch embroidery but, for the purposes of this book, stranded embroidery cotton has been used throughout (see main keys to projects).

As a general rule, however, the thread should be thin enough to slide through the holes of the canvas without distorting it, but also thick enough to cover the canvas beneath the stitches. Threads differ in thickness and weight depending on their 'ply' and 'strands'. A strand is a unit of thread and a ply is part of a strand. Threads are sold with different numbers of strands depending on their type. Those strands also have different numbers of plies. Strands can be separated from threads and used separately or in groups so you can vary the thickness you use.

Understanding the Charts and Keys

*E*ach of the symbols on the chart represents one cross stitch and the position of the stitch is counted on the fabric using the chart as a guide. Parts of the design may be outlined in back stitch; this is identified by the plain and dotted heavy lines around the stitch symbols.

The key tells you which symbol represents which colour, our models are stitched using the threads listed in the first column. As the alternatives are not always exact equivalents, it is advisable to check the colours by eye before you start stitching. For ease of working, we try to place each key next to its appropriate chart. When the chart and key appear on different pages, we give an additional mini key on the chart itself to show the number and symbol for each thread used.

It is possible that some colours appear twice in the key, normally you will still only require one skein. If more is required this will be noted. Other embroidery stitches, such as French knots, will be listed at the end.

The finished size tells you how many stitches high and wide your project will be. This, together with the information under Fabric and approximate finished design area, will help you decide on your fabric.

If you wish to use an alternative fabric, read Sizing Your Project on p. 10.

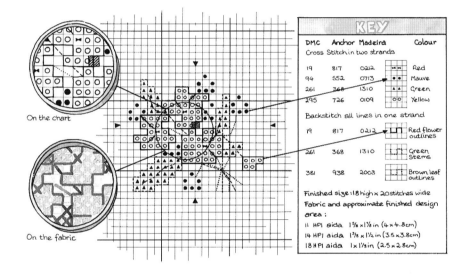

On the chart

On the fabric

DMC	Anchor	Madeira		Colour
Cross Stitch in two strands				
19	817	0212		Red
94	552	0713		Mauve
261	368	1310		Green
295	726	0109		Yellow
Backstitch all lines in one strand				
19	817	0212		Red flower outlines
261	368	1310		Green Stems
381	938	2003		Brown leaf outlines

Finished size: 18 high x 20 stitches wide
Fabric and approximate finished design area:
11 HPI aida 1⅝ x 1⅞ in (4 x 4.8cm)
14 HPI aida 1⅜ x 1½ in (3.5 x 3.8cm)
18 HPI aida 1 x 1⅛ in (2.5 x 2.8cm)

General Accessories

A good tapestry needle is essential and they come in various sizes from 13-26. The size of needle needed for each project is given in the key. Tapestry needles can be bought in packets of mixed sizes. Always change the needle for a new one when the surface begins to come off and the needle goes black.

A good pair of small embroidery scissors with sharp points are useful for cutting threads or snipping out 'mistakes'. Also, large dressmaking scissors are used for cutting the canvas to size before you stitch. They need to be strong as some canvas is quite stiff.

Other equipment that would be useful are a needlethreader, tweezers, thimble (optional), magnifier, flexible tape measure, pins and masking tape.

❀How to Prepare the Canvas for Stitching ❀

O nce you have chosen your canvas, threads and design you can now prepare to begin stitching. Cut the canvas along the threads to a square or rectangle remembering to add on at least two inches (five centimetres) all the way round the outside of the finished design area. Always work on a regular shaped piece of canvas whatever the shape of the design.

Bind the raw edges of the canvas with masking tape as this will prevent the thread from snagging on the edges and the canvas from unravelling. If it is a large project or one that will be stitched on for several months, then stitch fabric tape around the edges, as the masking tape will eventually come unstuck.

Fold the canvas lightly in half each way to find the centre and mark with a pencil. This is usually the best place to begin stitching.

Count the threads of the canvas out from the centre to find the outer edge of the design and mark the outline with a pencil or waterproof pen. This outline will be used later if you need to stretch your canvas back into shape when the stitching is completed. Place the canvas on to a piece of thick paper, such as blotting paper, and transfer the outline of the design onto this. The paper will be used as a stretching template once the project is complete. You will find this process invaluable later.

Sizing Your Project

$$\frac{\text{Number of stitches}}{\text{HPI of fabric}} = \text{size in inches}$$

W e give approximate finished design sizes wherever possible, but you may need to calculate how big a design will be on a different fabric. This is easy, just divide the number of stitches by the HPI of your fabric.

For example: if your project is 42 stitches high by 28 stitches wide and you are using 14HPI fabric, 42 divided by 14 makes 3in (7.5cm) high, and 28 divided by 14 makes 2in (5cm) wide. The only time this rule differs is for linen when you stitch over two threads. Use the same calculation but divide the HPI by two before you start.

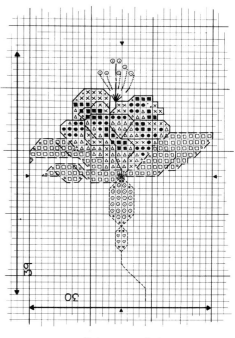

Sizing your project

Framing

T he urge to begin a new project can mean that you use an old, unsuitable frame or, worse still, that you are tempted to start working without one at all. Yet, to create even stitches, it is very important that the background fabric be kept taut.

Once you have chosen your project and gathered together the necessary materials, the first thing you must do is to mount your fabric. This can be achieved by using either a ring or a frame to hold your material.

Not everyone enjoys using a frame. However, you will find that it will stop nearly all the distortion that takes place while stitching, particularly if you are working on canvas.

Preparing the Fabric

M ost designs will recommend that you start stitching from the centre of the fabric. This will be indicated on your chart with arrows, but you will need to mark the centre of the material yourself.
Measure both sides of the fabric or gently fold it both ways to find the centre and then work two rows of basting (running) stitches both horizontally and vertically.

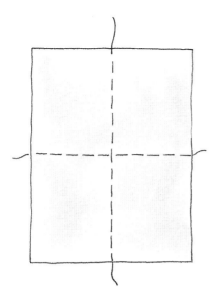

Finding the centre of your fabric

Over stitch (by hand or machine) or bind the edge of your material to prevent it fraying or catching your clothes.

Attaching your hoop or frame to a stand will give you both hands free. This enables you to put a hand on each side of the canvas or evenweave, and pass the needle through with ease.

When shopping for a new frame or hoop remember that designs and materials vary tremendously. Don't be tempted to buy the first one you are offered. You may be spending many hours at your project so it is important that you are comfortable. Stitching should be a pleasure.

Hoops

*H*oops can be used to hold most types of fabric. They come in many sizes and consist of two wooden or plastic rings which slot into one another. The size of the hoop must be adjusted so that the working area fits easily inside it.

Binding the Ring

To prevent the frame marking the fabric, bind the inner ring with tape or strips of material.

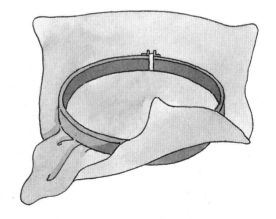

Binding the ring

Mounting

Place the fabric, design side up, over the smaller ring. Put the larger ring over the top and adjust the screw attachment. The larger ring should fit just over the top of the inner one and the fabric (illustration 1).

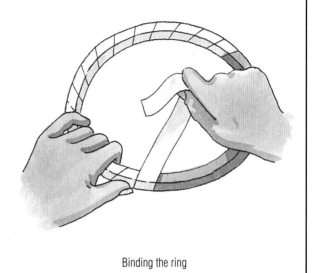

Illustration 1

Move your hands slowly around the hoop, pushing the outer ring down with the heel of the thumb, while pulling the fabric taut with finger and thumb (illust. 2). Adjust the screw to hold the fabric securely (illus. 4).

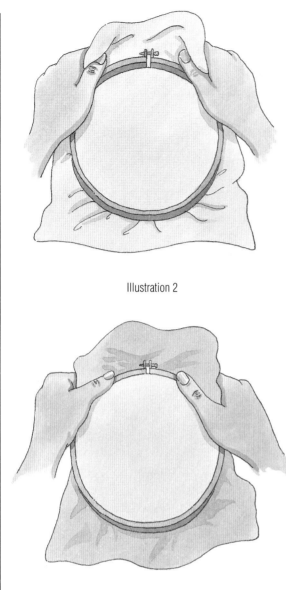

Illustration 2

Illustration 3

Straight-sided Frames

S traight-sided frames consist of two wooden stretcher bars at the side and two wooden rollers, with webbing attached to the top and bottom. The rollers are slotted into the stretchers and hold firmly by wing nuts, or a screw adjustment.

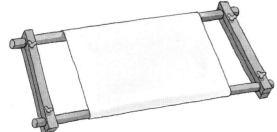

Straight-sided frame

Mounting

To dress your frame sew the top of the fabric to the top webbing and the bottom of the fabric to the bottom, keeping the fabric central to the webbing. Put the frame together and tighten the nuts to hold the fabric firmly in place. If the fabric is too long for the frame, wind the excess on to the roller until you need to work it.

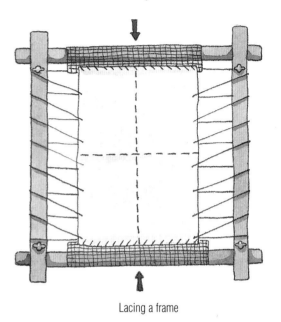

Lacing a frame

Lacing the sides of the frame will give an even working surface. Use strong thread, keep the fabric taut and attach the laces firmly to the frame. Side lacing is only recommmended if the whole of the area of working fabric is visible.

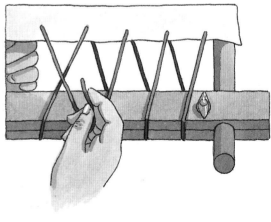

Lacing a frame

❧ The Stitches ❧

Cross Stitch

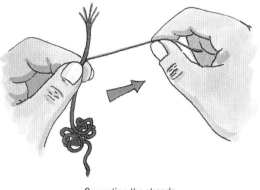

Separating the strands

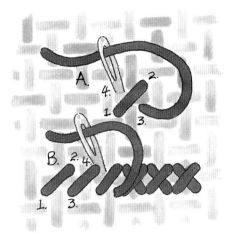

Cross stitch

Fold the fabric to find the centre.

Separate all six strands of your starting colour of stranded cotton. Then recombine two of them and thread the needle.

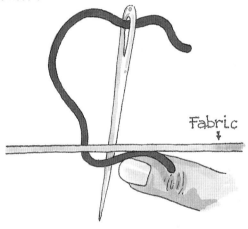

Fabric

Stitching the centre

Begin stitching at the centre of the design. Push the needle up through the fabric, hold the loose end and pull the thread through the fabric. Secure the loose end with your first few stitches.

Make one cross stitch for each symbol on the chart. Bring the needle up at 1, down at 2, up at 3 and down at 4.

For horizontal rows stitch all the way across, then work back. Finish off by weaving through the back of the stitches.

Using one strand of the cotton, add the back-stitches to outline the design.

Half Cross Stitch

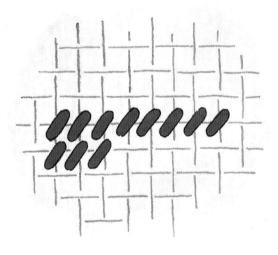

Half cross stitch

Work all the rows from left to right and, at the end of each one, finish the last stitch, leaving the needle at the back of the canvas.

Turn the canvas round and form the new row in line with the stitches just completed. Bring your needle up at 1, down at 2.

Three-quarter and Quarter Stitch

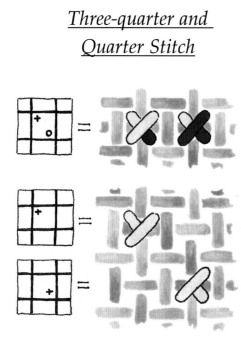

Three-quarter and quarter stitch

*I*f two symbols occupy one chart square, make the first half of the cross from bottom left to top right. Bring your needle out from the other corner and in at the centre. Work the quarter stitch from the remaining corner to the centre.

Long Stitch

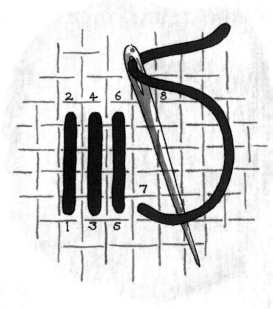

Long and short stitch

*L*ong stitch can be of any length, but you must be careful to check your tension if you make it too lon_ or the stitches will sag. Bring the needle out at 1, in at 2 out at 3 and in at 4.

French Knot

French knot

*T*o make a French knot, hold the thread and twist the needle round it twice. Partly push the needle into the fabric close to the emerging thread. Pull the thread until the knot tightens. Push the needle to the back.

❧ Finishing ❧

Washing Your Work

If necessary you can carefully wash your work in lukewarm water. If the colours begin to run, do not be tempted to stop rinsing until the bleeding has stopped.

Pad your ironing board with a towel and place a clean, thin cloth on top of it. Place the design wrong side up and carefully press - the thickness of the towel will stop you from ironing the stitching flat.

Iron the work until it's dry - make sure the iron isn't too hot or it will scorch the fabric. You are now ready to lace your work.

Lacing Your Work

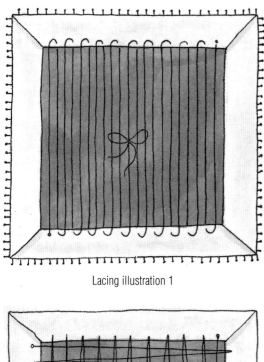

Lacing illustration 1

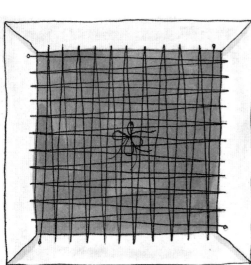

Lacing illustration 2

Place the work over the mountboard with the design in the centre, right side up.

Push pins along the top, going through the fabric and lightly into the board.

Pull the fabric gently and pin along the bottom in the same way. Repeat these instructions for each side.

Working from the back of the project, use a large-eyed needle, threaded with crochet cotton. Tie a knot at the end of your cotton and begin to lace from each side into the centre using a circular motion under and over (illustration 1). If you run out of thread before you reach the centre, join it with a reef knot.

Pull the crochet cotton rightly from each side and tie in the centre.

Repeat this for the other two sides (illustration 2).

Framing with a Flexi-Hoop

Framing with a flexi-hoop

Use the inside ring of the flexi-hoop as a template to cut out a felt backing disk.

Place the finished design centrally in the flexi-hoop.

Cut away any excess fabric, leaving about 1in (2.5cm) all the way round.

Make a row of stitches about ½in (13mm) in from the edge of the fabric. Then gather up tightly and secure the thread.

Place the felt backing disk over the back of the flexi-hoop and secure with a row of small running stitches on the edge.

Assembling a Card

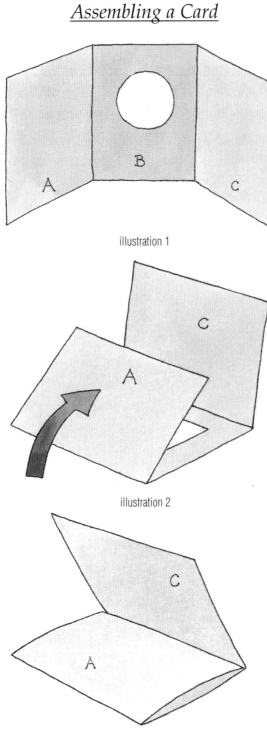

illustration 1

illustration 2

illustration 3

*P*lace a few strips of double-sided tape or spread a small amount of glue - Pritt Stick is ideal - on to the inside of B at the edges of the card (illustration 1).

Place your finished cross stitch face upwards on a flat surface. Turn your card over and hold it centrally above the stitched design. Press the card down on to the fabric until it holds firm (illustration 2).

Turn the card so that it is face down with the bottom of

the design towards you. Spread the glue or strips of double-sided tape on the outside edges of A. Firmly press A down on B (illustration 3).

If you are using glue keep a cloth handy to remove any excess. Place the finished card under a heavy weight to ensure that it holds securely. If you are using tape this will not be necessary.

Small Plastic Frames

*H*olding the frame in both hands, push out the clear plastic and snap-in back, with your thumbs.

Place the clear plastic centrally over your stitching and draw round it with a pencil.

Then cut around the line.

Now decide if you want to use a small piece of wadding behind your stitching or put the clear plastic in front instead. Whichever you choose, centre your fabric on the snap-in back and carefully push it into the frame. You may find it takes several attempts to centre the design, especially if you are using wadding.

Small plastic frame

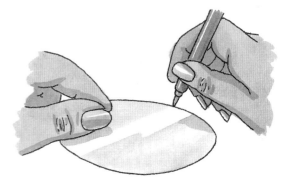

Small plastic frame

How to Assemble the Teddy Picture Frame

*I*f you intend to make the balloon bears into a picture frame, your stitches should be positioned centrally on the material size listed in the You Will Need box on page 88.

Using the line drawing as a guide, stitch the four sections of the chart to complete the rectangle.

Lay the design over the mount board and stitch a line of tacking stitches along the outside and inside edges of the frame using the mount as a guide.

The centre fabric section of the picture has to be removed, but it is important to leave enough material to fold over the back of the mount board. Cut from the centre point out to the row of tacking stitches at the four corners. Trim off some of the excess material.

Lay the wadding over the mount board, cutting a hole in the centre for the window.

Assemble the front section of the frame by laying the wadding over the mount board, and placing the stitching on top. Attach the material to the back of the board with double-sided tape. Pull the material firmly over the board and wadding, keeping the design as straight as possible.

The backboard should be covered with material, this can be evenweave or a toning fabric. Wrap your chosen frabric over the board and attach it to the wrong side with double-sided tape.

Tape your chosen picture behind the hold in the frame.

Assemble the front and back of the frame, using double-sided tape to hold it together. If you would like to hang your picture, place a piece of cord across the back of the frame with the ends between the mount boards. Using toning cotton, catch stitch the two edges of material together to complete the frame.

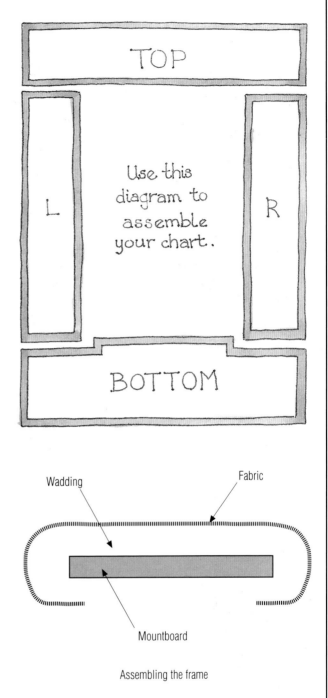

TOP

L

Use this diagram to assemble your chart.

R

BOTTOM

Wadding

Fabric

Mountboard

Assembling the frame

Country Comforts

Roses are red, violets are blue...an old valentine rhyme provides the inspiration for our two delicate flower panels.

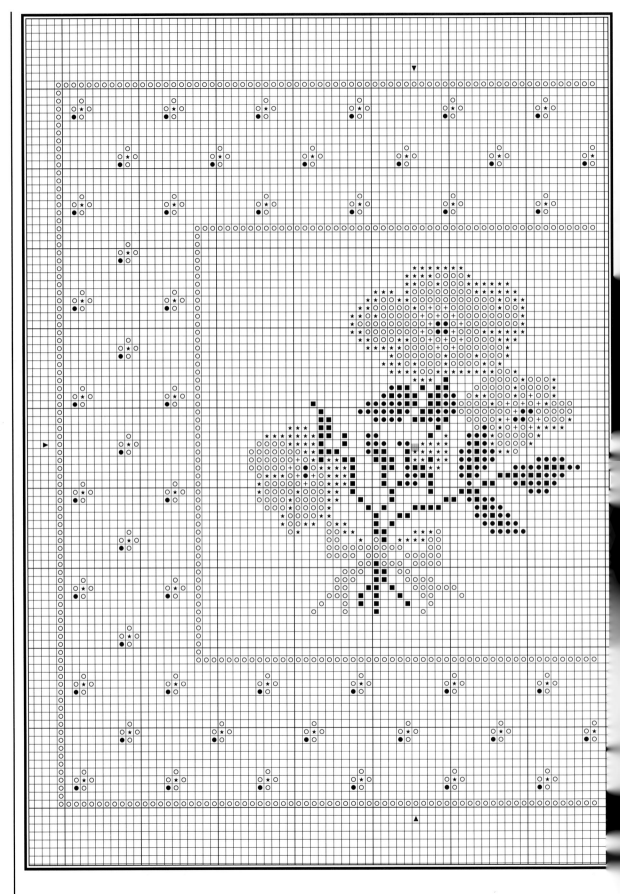

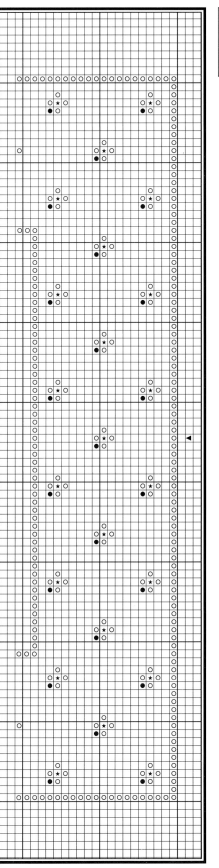

Dog Rose Cushion Key

DMC	Anchor	Madeira		Colour
Cross stitch in two strands				
726	295	0109	+ +	Yellow
962	052	0609	★ ★	Deep Pink
963	023	0608	○ ○	Pink
966	0206	1209	● ●	Green
988	243	1402	■ ■	Dark Green

Finished size: Stitch count 91 high x 91 wide
Fabric and approximate finished design area:
11 aida 8¼x8¼in (21x21cm)
14 aida 6½x6½in (16.5x16.5cm)
18 aida 5x5in (12.5x12.5cm)

You Will Need

For Each Flower Panel:

❀ 18HIP aida - 6x6in (15x15cm), white
❀ Stranded cotton - as listed in the key
❀ Tapestry needle - size 24
❀ Scissors

For Each Cushion:

❀ pad - 14x14in (35.5x35.5cm)
❀ Sewing equipment
❀ Graph paper
❀ Card
❀ Glue stick

❀ Pins
❀ Iron
❀ Pencil
❀ White crayoning pencil
❀ Ruler
❀ Fabrics (all washed and ironed)
  Patterned material -backing fabric - 1 square 14x14in (35.5x35.5cm)
  1 strip 2½x36in (6.5x91cm)
  Frill - 1 strip, 100x2½in (254x6.5cm) approx
  Plain material - 1 strip, 2½x48in (6.5x122cm)

Working Instructions

These two country-style cushions give you a chance to enjoy the beauty of nature indoors - perfect for the armchair gardener. Work the cross stitch in two strands. Wash and iron your finished design, carefully following the instructions given on page 15.

COUNTRY COMFORTS

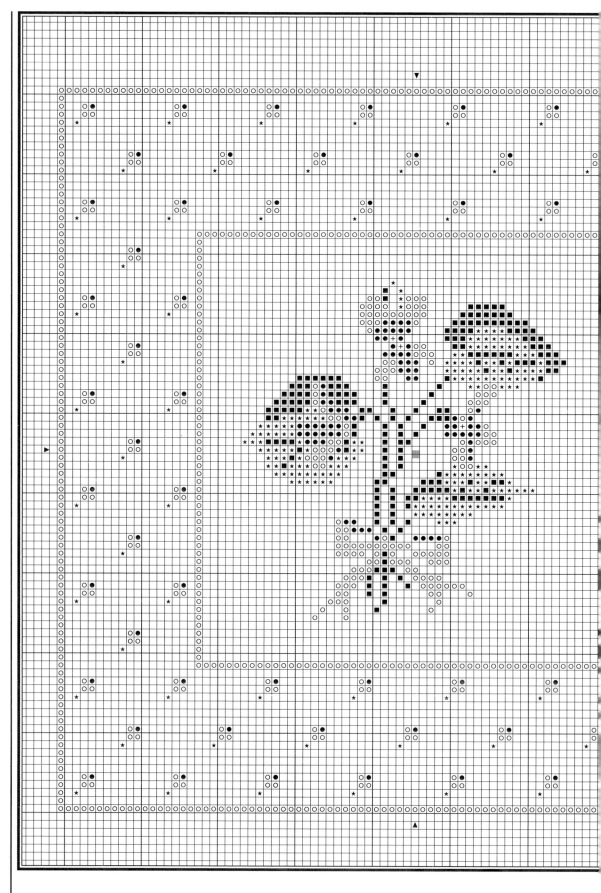

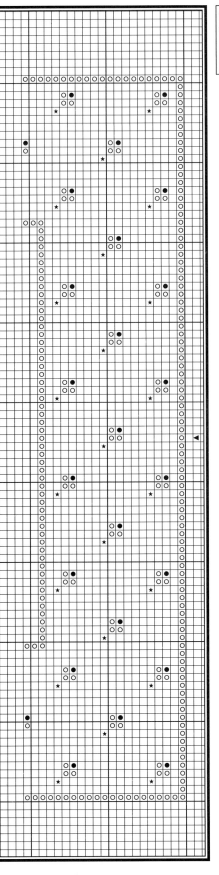

Violet Cushion Key

DMC	Anchor	Madeira			Colour
Cross stitch in two strands					
208	110	0804	●	●	Dark Violet
210	109	0803	○	○	Violet
726	295	0109	+	+	Yellow
3362	862	1514	■	■	Dark Green
3364	262	1603	★	★	Green

Finished size: Stitch count 91 high x 91 wide
Fabric and approximate finished design area:
11 aida 8¼x8¼in (21x21cm) 14 aida 6½x6½in (16.5x16.5cm) 18 aida 5x5in (12.5x12.5cm)

To Make Up the Cushion

When you have finished each panel, you can turn it into a luxurious cushion cover. Follow the instructions below to make the templates and fabric strips, then turn the page for the making up instructions.

Draw a 2 x 14in (5 x 35.5cm) rectangle accurately on to graph paper. The graph paper will ensure that the corners are square.

Cut out the shape on the outside of the drawn lines.

Stick the shape on to a piece of card and accurately cut along the drawn lines.

Lay your patterned fabric right-side down. The strip template should be placed on top, aligning the template with the straight grain of the fabric.

Draw around the card carefully in pencil or white crayon, whichever shows up best on your choice of fabric.

Cut ¼in (6mm) outside the pencil line.

How to Assemble the Cushion Front

Place your cross stitch design face-up on a flat surface.

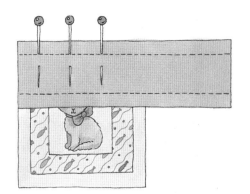

Pin a patterned strip to the centre square (your design) starting from the top left, aligning the edges with the right sides together. Pin through the pencil lines making sure that the pin comes out just outside the border of the design. Once on your second row the pins should emerge on the pencil line on the other piece of fabric.

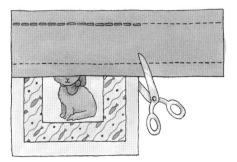

With a very small running stitch, or by machine, sew the two layers together along the drawn line. If you are sewing by hand, you can start with a knot and finish off with a firm back stitch.

Using the right-hand edge of the centre square as a guide, cut off any extra strip that sticks out beyond the square, then press the strip over to its right side. (It is important to press it each time, to maintain the accuracy in your work.)

Now turn the centre square anti-clockwise through 90 degrees and apply a second patterned strip in a similar way. Pinning and sewing as before, trim off excess and press open.

urn your work anti-clockwise to the next side and apply
third patterned strip, overlapping the previous strip.
in, sew, trim and open out.

Continue with one more patterned strip, before adding
ur plain strips. This will make a 14¼in (36.1cm)
quare including the ¼in turning on the outside edges.

Making and Attaching the Frill

Sew strips of patterned fabric together to form a
2½inx100in (6.5x255cm) strip. The ends are
then joined to form a complete circle (be careful
that the fabric isn't twisted).

Turn under ¼in (6mm) and then another ¼in
(6mm) on one long edge. Press and then
machine stitch into place.

On the other long edge, make two rows of
gathering stitches ¼in (6mm). Draw up the
threads to fit around the completed cushion front.

Place your cross stitch design face-up on the
table. Starting from the top left-hand corner, pin
and tack the gathered strip on to the design
aligning the edges. Both the frill and the cushion
front should be right sides together. Machine
stitch into place along the tacking line.

Lay the back of the cushion face up on the
table. On top of this, place the cushion front face
down. The frill should then be sandwiched
between the two layers of fabric.

Following the stitching already made when
attaching the frill, pin, then tack all three layers
together on this line. Leave a 7in (18cm) gap at
the bottom.

Turn the cushion cover through to the right
side.

Insert the cushion pad and sew up the gap with
small, neat stitches.

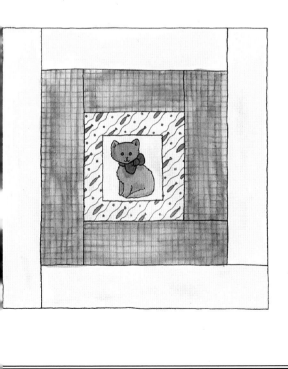

The Cat's Whiskers

❀ ❀ ❀

*Full of feline fun, our playful country cats are sure to delight
all cat lovers.*

Cat Sampler Key

Anchor	DMC	Madeira		Colour
Cross stitch in two strands				
001	White	White	⋈ ⋈	White
013	349	0212	▲ ▲	Deep Red
024	776	0503	◆ ◆	Light Pink
046	666	0210	△ △	Red
258	904	1413	♡ ♡	Grass Green
263	3051	1603	♥ ♥	Dark Grass Green
265	3348	1209	★ ★	Light Green
266	3347	1408	# #	Lime Green
267	469	1503	⁄ ⁄	Green
290	973	0105	⊠ ⊠	Yellow
304	971	0203	+ +	Orange
308	782	2212	∩ ∩	Ginger
357	801	2007	⊘ ⊘	Warm Brown
359	898	2006	⅄ ⅄	Chocolate
388	3033	1909	× ×	Pale Fawn
393	640	1905	○ ○	Beige
398	415	1802	□ □	Grey
403	310	Black	■ ■	Black
890	729	2209	z z	Sand
891	676	2208	I I	Pale Sand
3581	646	1811	≤ ≤	Brown

Backstitch all lines in one strand

403	310	Black	Black

French knots for the eyes in one strand

258	904	1413	Grass Green (Tortoiseshell)
265	3348	1209	Light Green (Kitten)
403	310	Black	Black (Eyes on Grey Cat)

Finished size: Stitch count 110 high x 80 wide
Fabric and approximate finished design area:
11 aida 10x 7¼ in 14 aida 7⅞ x 5¾ in
18 aida 6x 4½ in

For the Cat Designs You Will Need

❀ 14HPI aida - 12x10in (30.5x25.5cm), cream
❀ Stranded cotton - as listed in the key
❀ Tapestry needle - size 24
❀ Frame - 11x9in (28x23cm), green with gold rule
❀ Mounts - 9¾ x7¾ in (24.9x19.75cm) with a 7¾ x5¾ in (19.75x14.5cm) rectangular opening, green and red

Working Instructions

Cats and kittens make wonderful subjects and here are eight crazy cats to stitch as an unusual sampler, or to create as eight individual pictures.

Work the cross stitch in two strands.

The back stitch is then worked in one strand of black stranded cotton.

Stitch the cats' eyes in French knots - grass green for the tortoiseshell cat, light green for the kitten and black for the grey cat hanging from the branch.

Once all the stitching is complete, stitch over the top with cross stitch in two strands of orange - follow the chart below for the placement of the stitches.

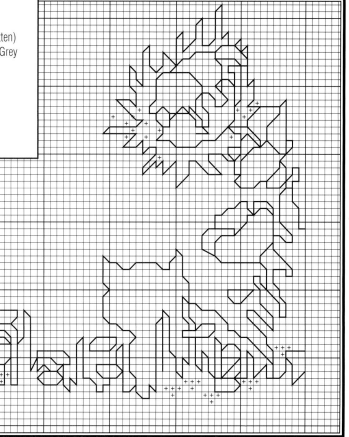

SNUG IN BED
BEFORE
I SLEEP
I COUNT
MY
DREAMLAND
FLOCK
OF SHEEP

Down a Country Lane

Take time to stitch our delightful country scenes, taken from walks along country lanes.

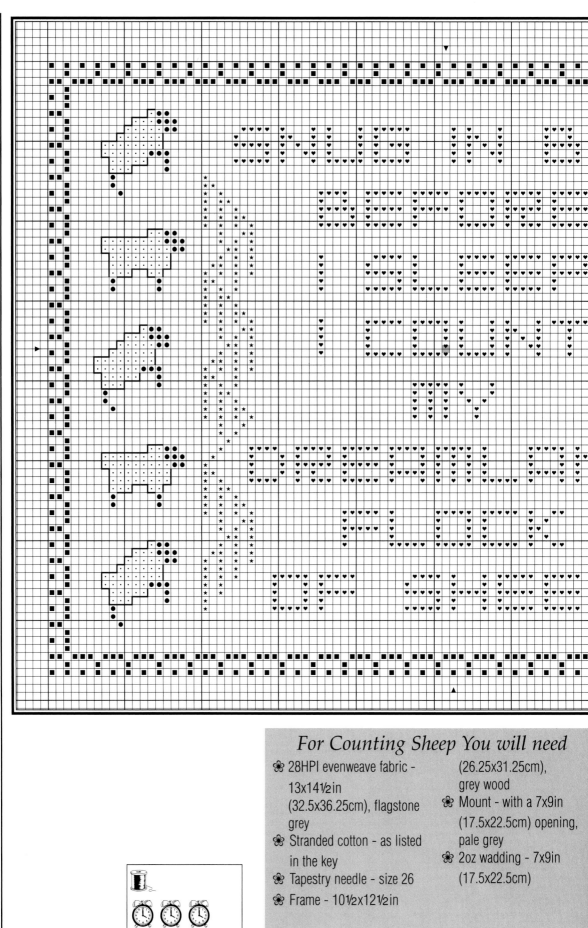

For Counting Sheep You will need

- 28HPI evenweave fabric – 13x14½in (32.5x36.25cm), flagstone grey
- Stranded cotton – as listed in the key
- Tapestry needle – size 26
- Frame – 10½x12½in
- (26.25x31.25cm), grey wood
- Mount – with a 7x9in (17.5x22.5cm) opening, pale grey
- 2oz wadding – 7x9in (17.5x22.5cm)

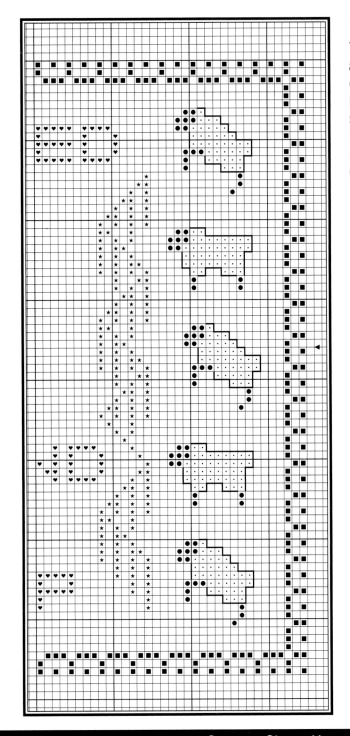

Working Instructions

These smaller projects are ideal to while away an evening, or to make as special gifts for friends and loved ones. All the projects are worked in two strands of stranded cotton, with one strand for the backstitch. Follow the instructions on pp.15-17 for making up the projects into cards and fitting into small frames.

Country Sheep Key

DMC	Anchor	Madeira			Colour
Cross stitch in two strands					
White	001	White	· ·	·	White
310	403	Black	● ●	●	Black
321	047	0510	♥ ♥	♥	Red
561	217	1205	■ ■	■	Dark green
733	280	1609	★ ★	★	Light green

Backstitch all lines in one strand

310	403	Black	⌐┐	Black sheep outlines

Our model was stitched using DMC threads; the Anchor and Madeira conversions are not necessarily exact colour equivalents.

Finished size: Stitch count 77 high x 105 wide
Fabric and approximate finished design area:
11HPI aida 7x9½in 14HPI aida5½x7½in
18HPI aida4¼x5¾in

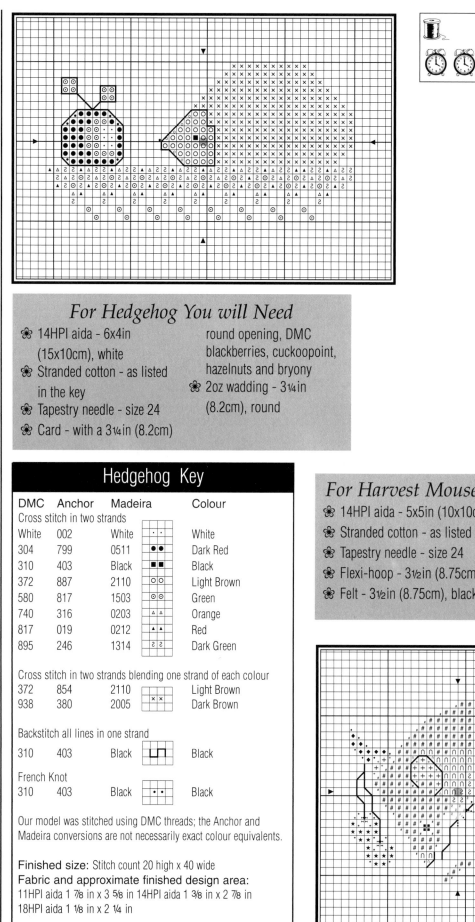

For Hedgehog You will Need

- ❀ 14HPI aida - 6x4in (15x10cm), white
- ❀ Stranded cotton - as listed in the key
- ❀ Tapestry needle - size 24
- ❀ Card - with a 3¼in (8.2cm) round opening, DMC blackberries, cuckoopoint, hazelnuts and bryony
- ❀ 2oz wadding - 3¼in (8.2cm), round

Hedgehog Key

DMC	Anchor	Madeira		Colour
Cross stitch in two strands				
White	002	White	· ·	White
304	799	0511	● ●	Dark Red
310	403	Black	■ ■	Black
372	887	2110	○ ○	Light Brown
580	817	1503	◎ ◎	Green
740	316	0203	△ △	Orange
817	019	0212	▲ ▲	Red
895	246	1314	z z	Dark Green
Cross stitch in two strands blending one strand of each colour				
372	854	2110		Light Brown
938	380	2005	× ×	Dark Brown
Backstitch all lines in one strand				
310	403	Black	⌐⌐	Black
French Knot				
310	403	Black	· ·	Black

Our model was stitched using DMC threads; the Anchor and Madeira conversions are not necessarily exact colour equivalents.

Finished size: Stitch count 20 high x 40 wide
Fabric and approximate finished design area:
11HPI aida 1 ⅞ in x 3 ⅝ in 14HPI aida 1 ⅜ in x 2 ⅞ in
18HPI aida 1 ⅛ in x 2 ¼ in

For Harvest Mouse You will need

- ❀ 14HPI aida - 5x5in (10x10cm), white
- ❀ Stranded cotton - as listed in the key
- ❀ Tapestry needle - size 24
- ❀ Flexi-hoop - 3½in (8.75cm) rope, black
- ❀ Felt - 3½in (8.75cm), black

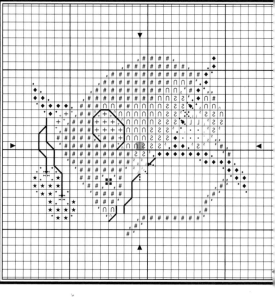

Squirrel Key

DMC	Anchor	Madeira		Colour
Cross stitch in two strands				
046	666	0210	◆ ◆	Red
358	433	2008	# #	Brown
387	822	2001	+ +	Light Beige
397	762	1804	∩ ∩	Light Grey
392	642	1905	2 2	Fawn
403	310	Black	■ ■	Black
683	319	1312	⋈ ⋈	Bottle Green
845	3011	1608	▲ ▲	Olive
905	3031	2003	♥ ♥	Dark Brown

DMC	Anchor	Madeira		Colour
Backstitch all lines in one strand				
358	433	2008		Brown body outline

DMC	Anchor	Madeira		Colour
392	642	1905		Fawn tail outlines
403	310	Black		Black nose & eye outlines

Our model was stitched using Anchor threads; the DMC and Madeira conversions are not necessarily exact colour equivalents.

Finished size: Stitch count 37 high x 31 wide
Fabric and approximate finished design area:
11HPI aida 3 3/8 in x 2 7/8 in 14HPI aida 2 5/8 in x 2 1/4 in
18HPI aida 2 in x 1 3/4 in

For Squirrel You will need

❈ 14HPI aida - 5x4in (12.5x10cm) white
❈ Stranded cotton - as listed in the key
❈ Tapestry needle -size 24
❈ Frame - 4x3in (10x7.5cm), gold
❈ 2oz wadding - 4x3in (10x7.5cm)

Harvest Mouse Key

Anchor	DMC	Madeira		Colour
Cross stitch in two strands				
002	White	White	· ·	White
019	817	0212	⋈ ⋈	Dark Red
046	666	0210	★ ★	Bright Red
049	3689	0607	∟ ∟	Pale Pink
301	744	0110	2 2	Yellow
313	402	0114	∩ ∩	Orange
369	435	2009	# #	Dark Tan
373	422	2103	+ +	Pale tan
380	839	1913	◆ ◆	Dark Brown
403	310	Black	■ ■	Black

Anchor	DMC	Madeira		Colour
Backstitch all lines in one strand				
49	3689	0607		Pale Pink Mouse Claws
371	433	2008		Very Dark Tan Cherry Stems & Harvest Mouse details

Our model was stitched using Anchor threads; the DMC and Madeira conversions are not necessarily exact colour equivalents.

Finished size: Stitch count 23 high x 28 wide
Fabric and approximate finished design area:
11HPI aida 2 in x 2 1/2 in 14HPI aida 1 5/8 in x 2 in
18HPI aida 1 1/4 in x 1 1/2 in

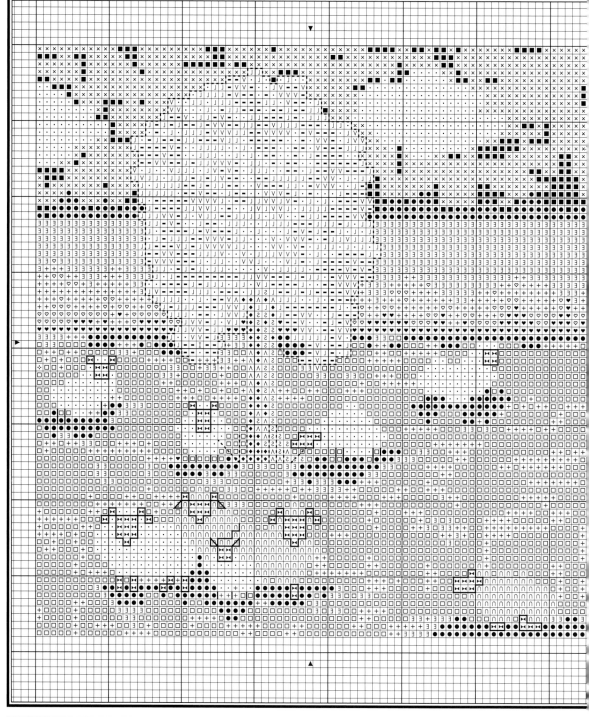

For Sheep in a Field You will need

❀ 14 HPI aida - 9½x9in (24.4x22.5cm), white

❀ Stranded cotton - as listed in the key

❀ Tapestry needle - size 24

❀ Frame - 7¾x7½in (19.4x18.75cm), pine

❀ Mount Board - with a 5½x5¼in (13.75x13.2cm) opening, black

❀ 2oz wadding - 5½x5¼in (13.75x13.2cm)

For Badger You will need

- ✿ 14HPI aida - 6x5in (15x12.5cm), cream
- ✿ Stranded cotton - as listed in the key
- ✿ Tapestry needle - size 24
- ✿ Flexi-hoop - 4½x3½in (11.25x8.75cm) oval, brown
- ✿ Felt - 4½x3½in (11.25x8.75cm) oval, brown
- ✿ 2oz wadding - 4½x3½in (11.25x8.75cm)

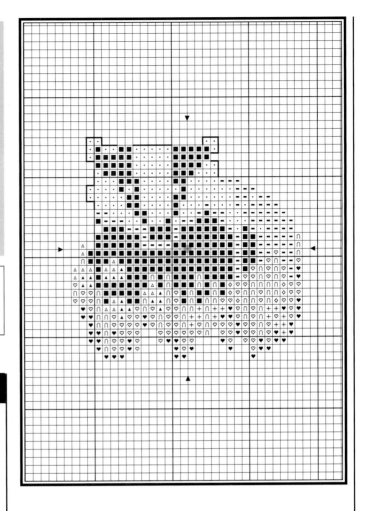

Sheep In a Field Key

DMC	Anchor	Madeira			Colour
Cross stitch in two strands					
White	002	White	·	·	White
Ecru	387	Ecru	∩	∩	Ecru
320	216	1311	▫	▫	Grass Green
367	217	1312	●	●	Green Shadow
433	370	2303	◆	◆	Dark Brown
702	226	1306	∧	∧	Leaf Green
776	024	0503	⌐	⌐	Dark Pink
818	048	0502	v	v	Light Pink
898	359	2006	−	−	Mid Brown
3021	382	1810	s	s	Light Brown
3325	140	1002	×	×	Light Blue
3345	268	1406	♥	♥	Dark Green
3346	257	1504	♡	♡	Mid Green
3347	266	1408	+	+	Light Green
3348	265	1209	∃	∃	Light Green
3755	145	1013	■	■	Dark Blue
3799	236	1713	◄	◄	Dark Grey

Backstitch all lines in one strand

900	333	0208	Leaf Green tree outlines & grass
3799	236	1713	Dark Grey sheep outlines

Our model was stitched using DMC threads; the Anchor and Madeira conversions are not necessarily exact colour equivalents.

Finished size: Stitch count 78 high x 75 wide
Fabric and approximate finished design area:
11HPI aida 7 in x 6 ⅞ in 14HPI aida 5 ½ in x 5 ⅜ in
18HPI aida 4 ⅜ in x 4 ⅛ in

Badger Key

DMC	Anchor	Madeira			Colour
Cross stitch in two strands					
002	White	White	·	·	White
011	3705	0214	▲	▲	Light red
046	666	0210	▲	▲	Red
130	799	1004	+	+	Light Blue
131	798	0911	◇	◇	Blue
225	703	1307	∩	∩	Light Green
245	986	1405	♡	♡	Mid Green
263	935	1505	♥	♥	Dark Green
399	318	1801	−	−	Grey
403	310	Black	■	■	Black

Backstitch all lines in one strand

399	318	1801	Grey

Our model was stitched using Anchor threads; the DMC and Madeira conversions are not necessarily exact colour equivalents.

Finished size: Stitch count 28 high x 30 wide
Fabric and approximate finished design area:
11HPI aida 2 ½ in x 2 ¾ in 14HPI aida 2 in x 2 ⅛ in
18HPI aida 1 ½ in x 1 ⅝ in

Down to a Fine Art

Translate the skill and artistry of botanical watercolours to silken threads and fine fabric with this elegant study of the beautiful Rhododendron 'Unique'.

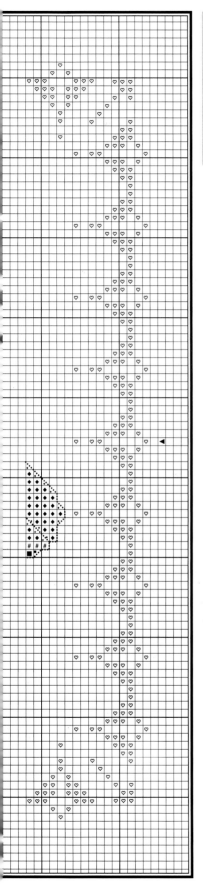

For the Rhododendron You Will Need

❀ 30HPI Murano - 13x12in (33x30.5cm), mushroom
❀ Stranded cotton - as listed in the key
❀ Tapestry needle - size 26
❀ Frame - 11½x10¾in (29.3x 27.4cm) green-stained wood
❀ Mounts - 10½x9¾in (26.5x24.9cm), pale green and white, with a 6½x5¾ in (16.5x23.6cm) rectangle cut from the centre

Rhododendron Key

Cross stitch in two strands except for the border which is worked in one strand

Anchor	DMC	Madeira		Colour
002	White	White	· ·	White
214	503	1310	♡ ♡	Light green
216	320	1311	◆ ◆	Medium green
217	561	1312	# #	Dark green
218	501	1313	■ ■	Very dark green
234	3072	1709	○ ○	Light grey
235	317	1801	▲ ▲	Medium grey
292	746	0101	× ×	Lemon
306	725	0113	★ ★	Orange
398	415	1803	⊙ ⊙	Grey
893	761	0813	∩ ∩	Light pink
894	223	0812	⋈ ⋈	Pink
895	316	0809	♥ ♥	Dark pink

Backstitch all lines in one strand

269	936	1507		Dark green outline leaves and lettering
400	317	1714		Grey detail on flowers
401	844	1809		Dark grey outline flowers

French knot in one strand

| 269 | 936 | 1507 | | Dark green dot on 'i' of unique |

Finished size: Stitch count 95 high x 86 wide
Fabric and approximate finished design area:
11 aida 8⅝x7¾ in 14 aida 6¾x6⅛in 18 aida 5¼x4¾in

Working Instructions

Work the cross stitch on the flowers and leaves in two strands of stranded cotton. Stitch the border in one strand over two threads of fabric.

The back stitch is worked in one strand of cotton: dark green for the lettering and leaf outlines, dark grey to outline the flowers and grey for the detail on the flower. Dot the 'i' in 'unique' with a French knot in one strand of dark green.

This project was designed with Anchor threads. We give alternatives, but these are from a conversion chart and should be checked by eye.

This is a complicated design and is best worked on a finer fabric, stitched over two threads. Your project can be completed on aida, but you should be prepared for the difficulty of working a large number of quarter stitches.

Country Nightlife

❋❋❋

The countryside becomes alive at night with owls and pussycats stalking their prey.

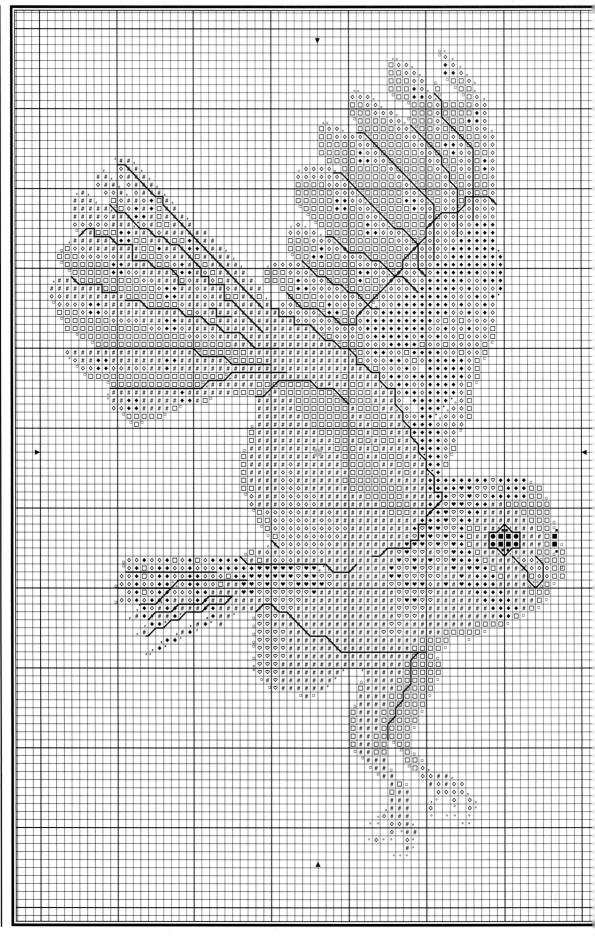

Working Instructions

Why not try stitching one of our nightime friend designs to while away an evening? All the projects are worked in two strands of stranded cotton, with one strand for the backstitch. Follow the instructions on pp.15-17 for making up the projects into cards and fitting into small frames.

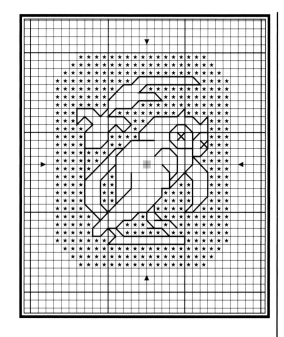

For the Big Owl
You will Need

❀ 14HPI aida - 3x3in (7.5x7.5cm), cream
❀ Stranded cotton - as listed in the key
❀ Tapestry needle - size 24
❀ Gold effect frame - 2½x2½in (6.5x6.5cm)
❀ 2oz wadding 2¼x2¼in (5.7x5.7cm)

For the Red Owl
You will need

❀ 14HPI aida - 13x12in (33x30.5cm), black
❀ Stranded cotton - as lsited in the key
❀ Tapestry needle - size 24
❀ Frame - 12x10¾in (30.5x27cm), black
❀ Mount - with a 9¼x7¼in (23.5x18.5cm) oval opening, white

Big Owl Key

DMC	Anchor	Madeira		Colour
Cross stitch in two strands				
White	002	White	□ □	White
300	357	2304	♥ ♥	Medium Brown
310	403	Black	■ ■	Black
317	400	1714	● ●	Dark Grey
415	398	1802	# #	Light Grey
951	881	2308	◇ ◇	Light Brown
3031	360	2006	◆ ◆	Deep Brown
3776	326	2302	▽ ▽	Orange Brown
Backstitch all lines in one strand				
310	403	Black		Black

Finished size: Stitch count 103 high x 67 wide
Fabric and approximate finished design area:
11 aida 9 3⁄8 in x 6 in 14 aida 7 3⁄8 in x 4 3⁄4 in
18 aida 5 3⁄4 in x 3 3⁄4 in.

Red Owl Key

Anchor	DMC	Madeira		Colour
Cross stitch in two strands				
9046	817	0202	✷ ✷	Red
Backstitch all lines in two strands				
403	310	Black		Black

Finished size: Stitch count 27 high x 23 wide
Fabric and approximate finished design area:
11 aida 2½x2⅛in 14 aida 2x1⅝in
18 aida 1½x1¼in

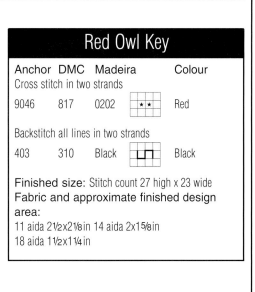

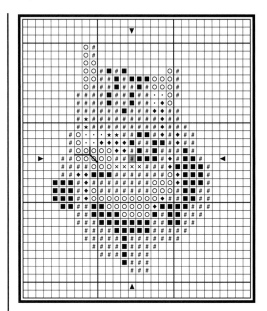

Black and Grey Cat Key

DMC	Anchor	Madeira		Colour
Cross stitch in two strands				
White	001	White	○○	White
318	399	1801	# #	Light grey
798	131	0911	★ ★	Bright blue
932	920	0710	◆ ◆	Blue grey
950	881	2309	· ·	Pink
3799	236	1713	■ ■	Dark grey
Backstitch all lines in one strand				
3799	236	1713	⌐⌐	Dark grey

Finished size: Stitch count 29 high x 21 wide
Fabric and approximate finished design area:
11 aida 2⅝x2in 14 aida 2x1½in
18 aida 1⅝x1¼in

For the Black and Grey Cat You will need

❀ 14HPI aida - 4x4in (10x10cm), light blue
❀ Stranded cotton - as listed in the key
❀ Tapestry needle - size 24
❀ Flexi-hoop - 2½in (6.5cm), round, light blue
❀ Felt - 2½in (6.5cm), round, light blue

For the Lucky Black Cat You will need

❀ 14HPI aida - 6x4in (15x10cm), cream
❀ Stranded cotton - as listed in the key
❀ Tapestry needle - size 24
❀ Card - poppies and corn (DMC)
❀ 2oz wadding - 3¾x3in, (9.5x7.5cm)

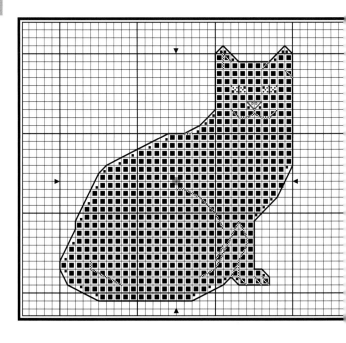

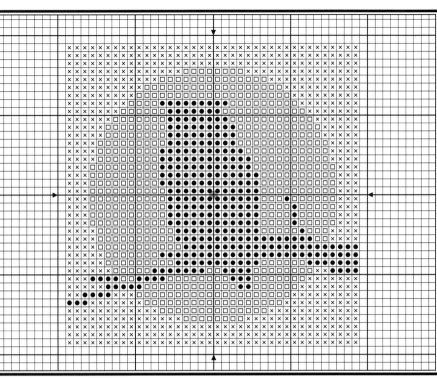

Owl in the Moon Key

DMC	Anchor	Madeira		Colour
Cross stitch in three strands				
310	403	Black	● ●	Black
Cross stitch in two strands				
762	397	1804	□ □	Light grey
930	922	1712	× ×	Blue

Finished size: Stitch count 38 square
Fabric and approximate finished design area:
11 aida 3½in square 14 aida 2¾in square
18 aida 2⅛in square

Lucky Black Cat Key

DMC	Anchor	Madeira		Colour
Cross stitch in three strands				
310	403	Black	■ ■	Black
907	255	1410	★ ★	Green
945	868	0305	◉ ◉	Flesh pink
Backstitch all lines in two strands				
White	001	White		White body detail & mouth
310	403	Black		Black outline & pupils
907	255	1410		Green eyes
945	868	0305		Flesh pink nose

Finished size: Stitch count 32 high x 30 wide
Fabric and approximate finished design area:
11 aida 2⅞x2¾in 14 aida 2¼x2⅛in
18 aida 1¾x1⅝in

For the Owl in the Moon You will need

❀ 14HPI aida - 5½x5½in (14x14cm), cream
❀ Stranded cotton - as listed in the key
❀ Tapestry needle - size 24
❀ Photoframe - 4x4in (10x10cm), white and gold
❀ 2oz wadding - 3¼x3¼in (8.8cm)

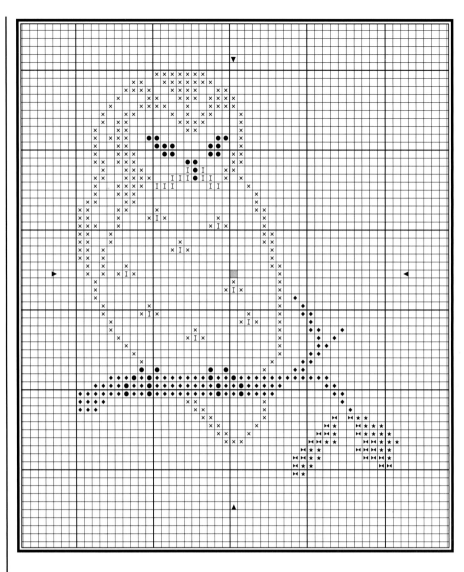

Branch Owl Key

Anchor	DMC	Madeira		Colour
Cross stitch in two strands				
036	761	0813	I I	Light gold
215	368	1310	⋈ ⋈	Medium green
217	561	1205	★ ★	Dark green
358	433	2008	× ×	Brown
381	938	2003	● ●	Dark brown
858	524	1511	◆ ◆	Moss green

Finished size: Stitch count 51 high x 42 wide
Fabric and approximate finished design area:
11 aida 4⅝x3¾in 14 aida3⅝x3in
18 aida 2⅞x2⅜in

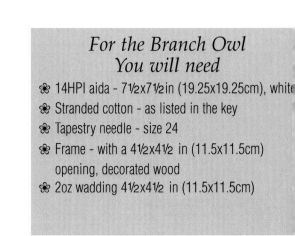

*For the Branch Owl
You will need*

❀ 14HPI aida - 7½x7½in (19.25x19.25cm), white
❀ Stranded cotton - as listed in the key
❀ Tapestry needle - size 24
❀ Frame - with a 4½x4½ in (11.5x11.5cm)
  opening, decorated wood
❀ 2oz wadding 4½x4½ in (11.5x11.5cm)

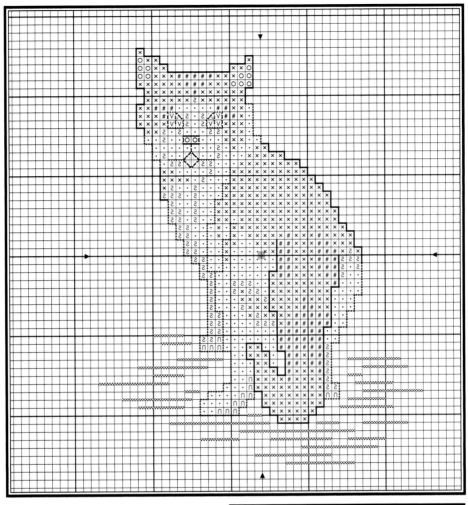

Black and White Cat Key

Anchor	DMC	Madeira			Colour
Cross stitch in two strands					
002	White	White	·	·	White
236	413	1713	×	×	Dark Grey
281	731	1613	o	o	Olive Green
392	3023	1903	#	#	Fawn
397	762	1804	v	v	Pale Grey
403	310	Black	s	s	Black
882	407	2310	n	n	Flesh

Anchor	DMC	Madeira		Colour
Backstitch all lines in one strand				
236	413	1713		Dark Grey face details
266	471	1408		Green ground
403	310	Black		Black body outlines
8581	646	1811		Mid-Grey body outlines

Finished size: Stitch count 47 high x 42 wide
Fabric and approximate finished design area:
11 aida 4 1/4 in. x 3 7/8 in. 14 aida 3 3/8 in. x 3 in.
18 aida 2 5/8 in. x 2 3/8 in.

For the Black and White Cat You will need

❀ 18HPI aida - 5x4in (12.5x10cm), cream
❀ Stranded cotton - as listed in the key
❀ Tapestry needle - size 26
❀ Oval frame - 4 1/4 x 3 1/4 in (11x8cm), gold effect
❀ 2oz wadding - 4 1/4 x 3 1/4 in (11x8cm)

Summer in the Meadow

Capture the very essence of the season with this unusual A-Z summer sampler, every letter is alive with butterflies and wild flowers.

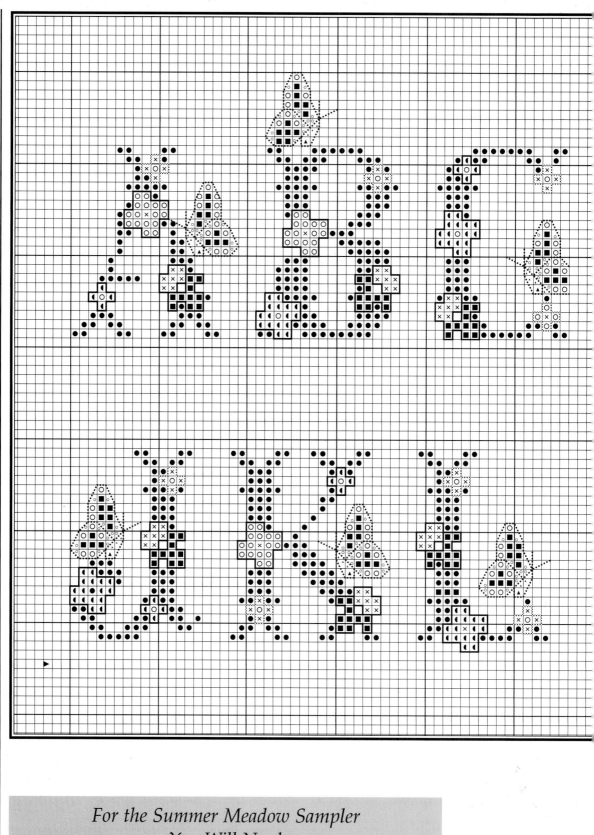

For the Summer Meadow Sampler
You Will Need

❊ 30HPI linen - 14x19in (35.5x48cm),
  off-white
❊ Stranded cotton - as listed in the key

❊ Tapestry needle - size 26
❊ Frame - 14x17in (35.5x43cm), gold

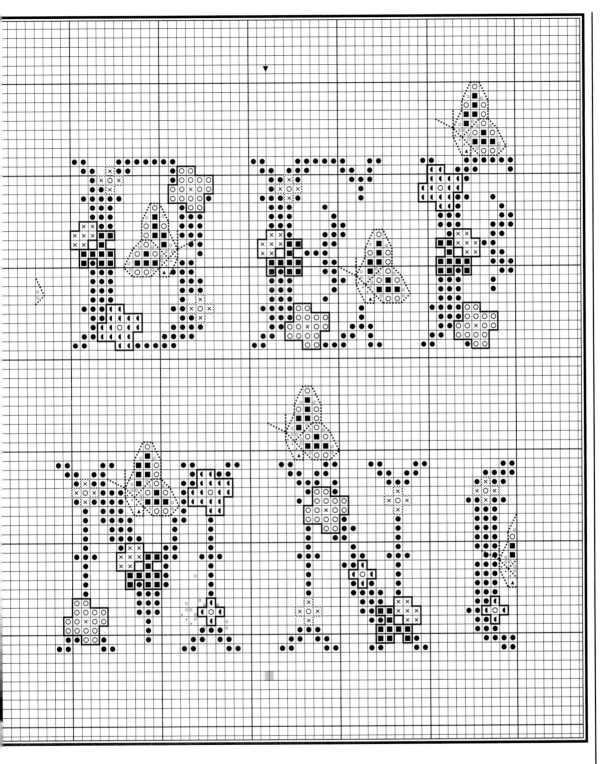

Working Instructions

This project was designed for a finer fabric where each cross is worked over two threads. Your project can be completed on aida but you should be prepared for the difficulty of working a large number of quarter stitches.

The cross stitch is worked in two strands over two threads of linen.

The back stitch is worked in one strand - rich brown for the butterflies, brown for the birds and ground below the gate, purple and green for the flowers and green for the tufts of grass.

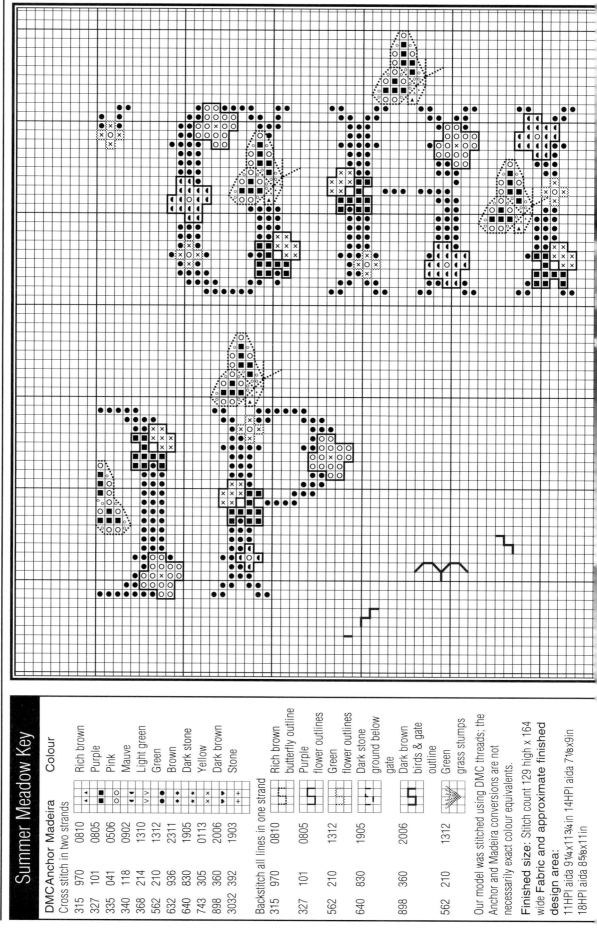

Summer Meadow Key

DMC Anchor Madeira
Cross stitch in two strands

DMC	Anchor	Madeira		Colour
315	970	0810		Rich brown
327	101	0805		Purple
335	041	0506		Pink
340	118	0902		Mauve
368	214	1310		Light green
562	210	1312		Green
632	936	2311		Brown
640	830	1905		Dark stone
743	305	0113		Yellow
898	360	2006		Dark brown
3032	392	1903		Stone

Backstitch all lines in one strand

315	970	0810	Rich brown butterfly outline
327	101	0805	Purple flower outlines
562	210	1312	Green flower outlines
640	830	1905	Dark stone ground below gate
898	360	2006	Dark brown birds & gate outline
562	210	1312	Green grass stumps

Our model was stitched using DMC threads; the Anchor and Madeira conversions are not necessarily exact colour equivalents.

Finished size: Stitch count 129 high x 164 wide **Fabric and approximate finished design area:**
11HPI aida 9¼x11¾in 14HPI aida 7⅛x9in
18HPI aida 8⅝x11in

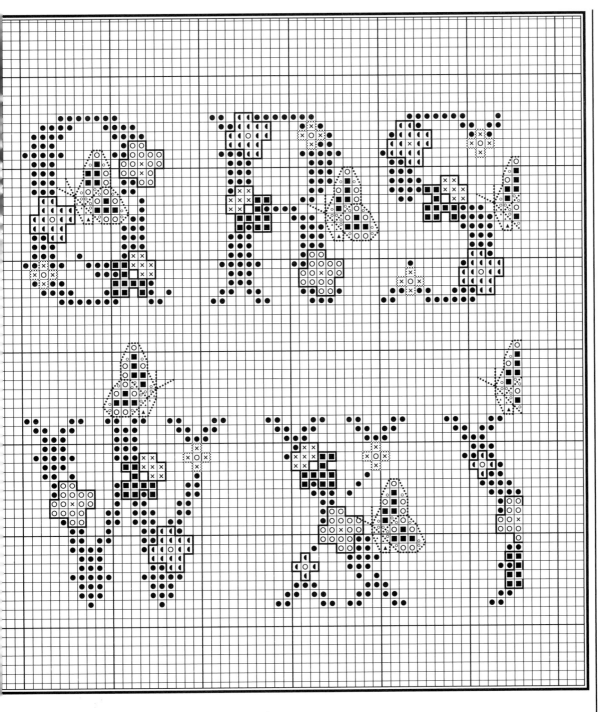

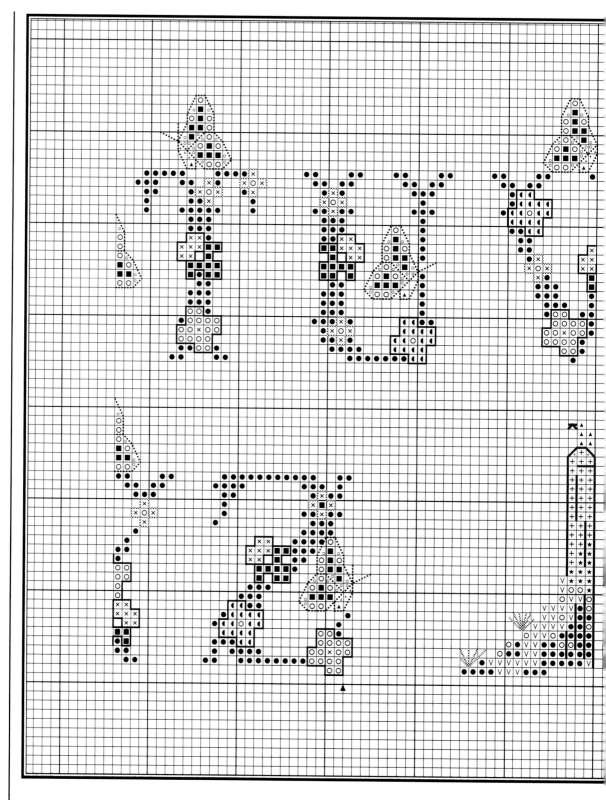

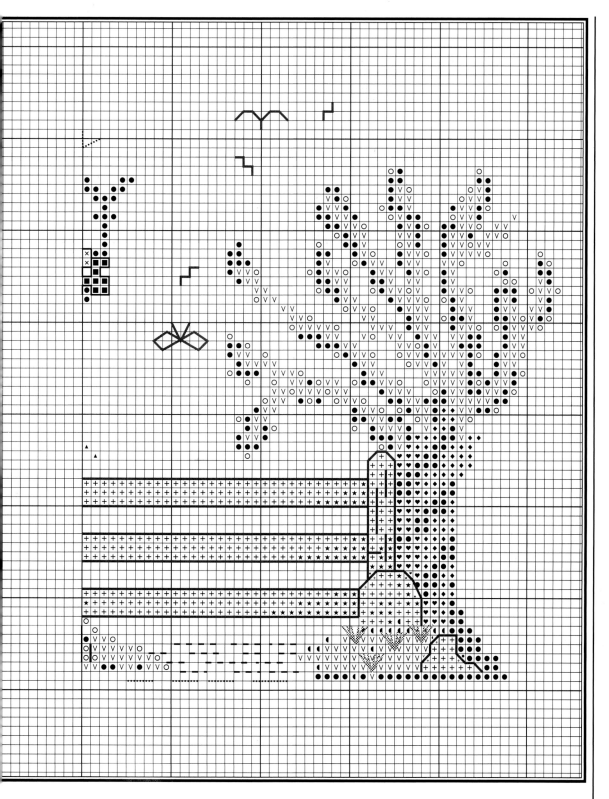

Wish you Were Here

Building sandcastles, collecting shells, going on donkey rides - re-live the fun of childhood holidays with this enchanting seaside frieze.

For Wish you Were Here You Will Need

- ❀ 14HPI aida - 6x16in (15x40.5cm), white
- ❀ Stranded cotton - as listed in the key
- ❀ Tapestry needle - size 24
- ❀ Frame - 5¾x 15½in (14.5x39.3cm), wood-effect, with gold rule
- ❀ Mounts - 5¼x15in (13.1x38cm), red, with a 2¾x12¾in (6.9x32.5cm) rectangular opening

Working instructions

Work the cross stitch in two strands of stranded cotton.

The backstitch is worked in two strands of dark sea green for the waves, and two strands of black for the bucket handle. The girl's mouth is worked in one strand of red and the rest of the design is back stitched in one strand of black.

Work the girl's and dog's eyes in French knots with one strand of black.

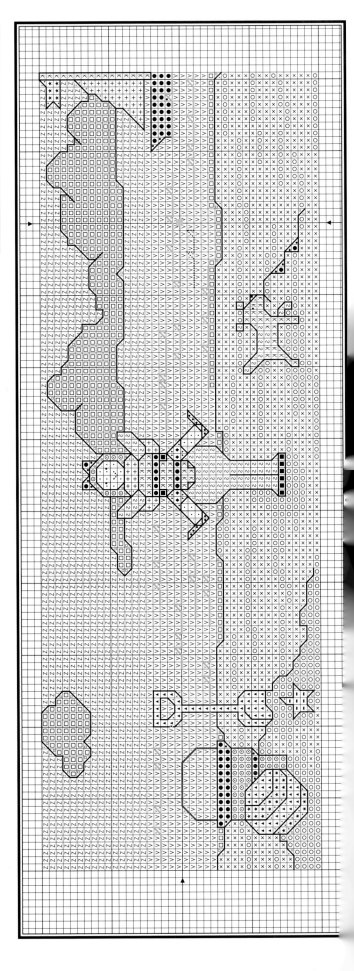

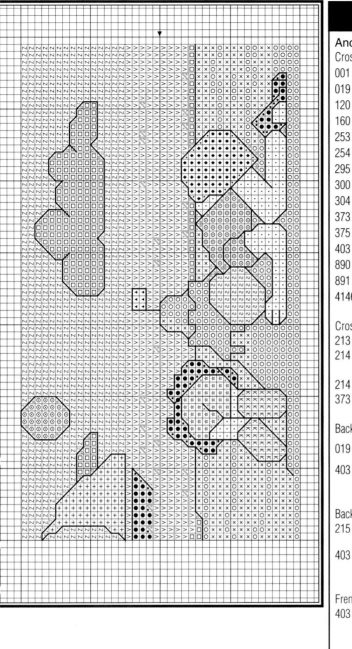

Wish you were here Key

Anchor	DMC	Madeira		Colour
Cross stitch in two strands				
001	White	White	□□	White
019	321	0510	●●	Red
120	794	0907	z z	Sky blue
160	813	1013	♦ ♦	Blue
253	472	1414	★ ★	Light lime green
254	907	1410	☆ ☆	Lime green
295	726	0109	⊙⊙	Yellow
300	745	0111	+ +	Cream
304	741	0201	▲ ▲	Orange
373	436	2011	K K	Light brown
375	420	2104	ƨ ƨ	Dark brown
403	310	Black	■■	Black
890	729	2209	○○	Dark sand
891	676	2208	× ×	Light sand
4146	948	0306	· ·	Flesh

Cross stitch using one strand of each colour				
213	369	1309	v v	Light green
214	368	1310		Green

214	368	1310		Green
373	436	2011	- -	Light brown

Backstitch in one strand				
019	321	0510		Red mouth
403	310	Black		Black outlines and details on design

Backstitch in two strands				
215	320	1311		Dark green waves
403	310	Black		Black bucket handles

French knots using one strand				
403	310	Black	· ·	Black eyes for girl and dog

Finished size: Stitch count 40 high x 180 wide
Fabric and approximate finished design area:
11 aida 35⁄8 x 163⁄8 in
14 aida 27⁄8 x 127⁄8 in
18 aida 21⁄8 x 10 in

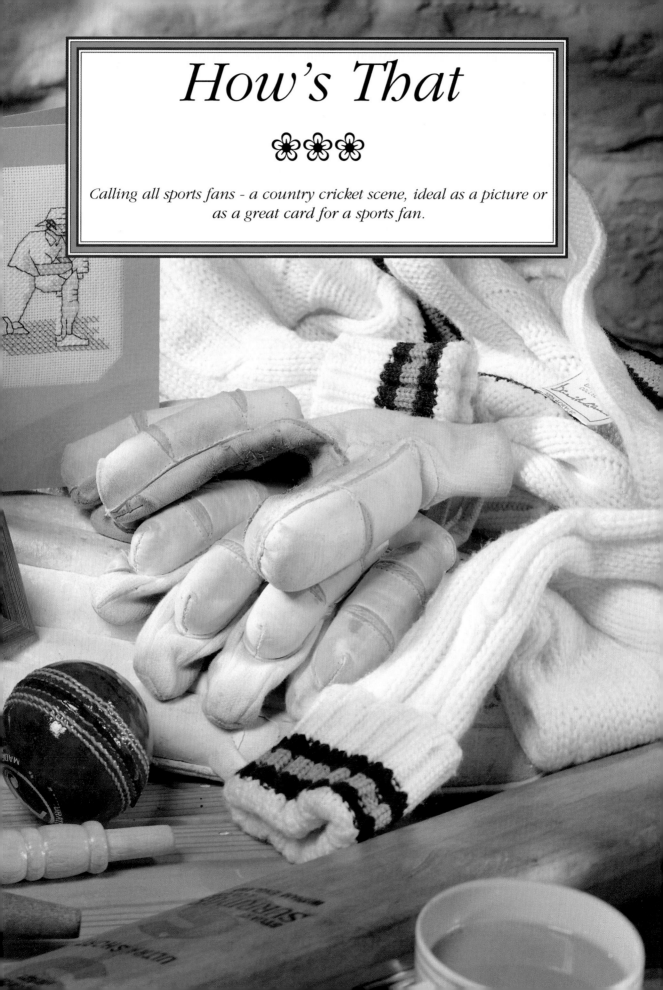

How's That

❀ ❀ ❀

Calling all sports fans - a country cricket scene, ideal as a picture or as a great card for a sports fan.

How's That Key

DMC	Anchor	Madeira		Colour
Cross stitch in one strand				
White	001	White	◆ ◆	White
402	347	2307	– –	Flesh
640	393	1905	@ @	Dark flesh
838	381	1914	2 2	Brown
902	072	0601	★ ★	Red brown
3347	266	1408	× ×	Light green
3362	862	1514	■ ■	Dark green
Cross stitch in two strands				
White	001	White	· ·	White
402	347	2307	o o	Flesh
453	281	1806	# #	Grey
902	072	0601	★ ★	Red brown
Backstitch in number of strands indicated in brackets				
White	001	White		White(2)cloud outline
902	072	0601		Red brown(2)corner detail and cricket ball
3362	862	1514		Dark green(1) horizon line
838	381	1914		Brown outline of cricketer(1), letters and birds(2)
793	121	0906		Blue(1) sky detail
White	001	White		White(1) leg pads(these are worked in two stitch lengths to fill the area in the direction indicated)

Finished size: Stitch count 170 high x120 wide
Fabric and approximate finished design area:
18 aida 4¾x3⅜ in (12x8.5cms) 18 aida worked over two threads
9⅜x6¾ in (24x17cms)

For How's That You Will Need

❀ 18HPI Zweigart Rustico aida - 13x11in (33x28cm)
❀ Stranded cotton - as listed in the key
❀ Tapestry needle - size 26
❀ Frame - 11½x9in (29.3x23cm) dragged wooden frame, gold edge

Working Instructions

Cross stitch the following areas in one strand: the cricketer's face, hair and arms are worked in three shades of flesh and brown. The grass and trees are worked in two shades of green, and the cloud detail in white. Work the four cricket balls on the corners in red-brown.

Cross stitch the following areas in two strands: the cricketer's clothing is worked in white and grey. The bat and wicket are in flesh and the three border rows in red-brown.

Back stitch the following areas in one strand: the horizon is worked in one strand of green. The cricketer and wicket are outlined in one strand of brown and the sky is back stitched in one strand of blue.

Back stitch the following areas in two strands: the leg pads are filled in with two strands of white in the direction shown on the chart. The clouds are outlined in two strands of white. The cricket balls are outlined in two strands of red-brown while the birds and lettering are worked in two strands of brown.

The Bear Essentials

Bring back those fond memories of childhood friends, with our delightful collection of teddy bears to suit all abilities.

Teddy Heart Key

DMC	Anchor	Madeira		Colour
Cross stitch in two strands				
422	373	2103		Gold
746	386	0101		Light Ecru
761	036	0813		Pink
898	359	2006		Dark Brown
920	339	0401		Medium Brown
Backstitch all lines in one strand				
310	403	Black		Black

Finished size: Stitch coun t28 high x 30 wide
Fabric and approximate finished design area:
11 aida 2½ in. x 2 ¾ in. 14 aida 2 in. x 2 ⅛ in.
18 aida 1 ½ in. x 1 ⅝ in.

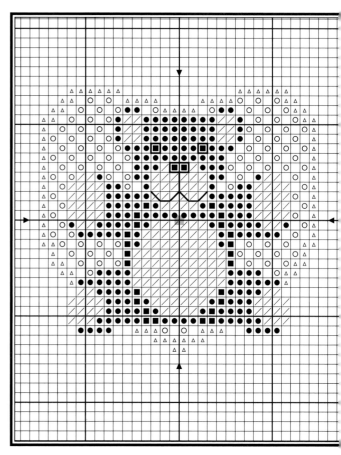

For Teddy Heart You Will Need

❀ 18HPI aida - 11x9in (28x23cm), cream
❀ Stranded cotton - as listed in the key
❀ Tapestry needle - size 26
❀ Frame 9½x8in (24.5x120.5cm), pine
❀ Mount Board - with a 6¼x5in
  (15.75x12.5cm) rectangular opening
❀ 2oz wadding - 6¼x5in (15.75x12.5cm)

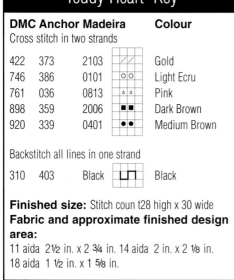

For Grandma's Bear You Will Need

❀ 14HPI aida - 5x4in (12.5x10cm), white
❀ Stranded cotton - as listed in the key
❀ Tapestry needle - size 24
❀ Flexi-hoop - 4x3in (10x7.5cm) red, oval

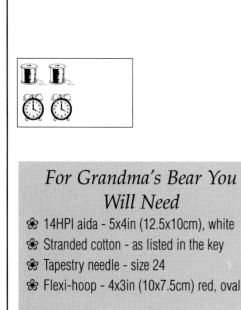

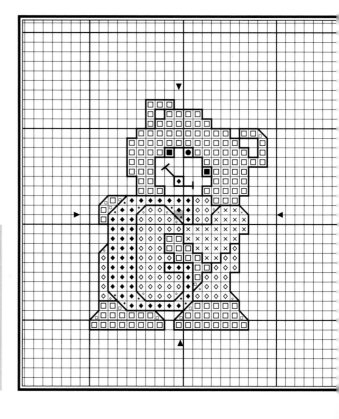

Working Instructions

A selection of teddy bears to while away the time or to make up as special gifts. All the projects are worked in two strands of stranded cotton, with one strand for the back stitch.

Unless otherwise indicated, follow the instructions on pp. 15-17 for making up the projects into cards and fitting into small frames.

For Teddy Bridesmaid You Will Need

❀ 14HPI aida - 6x4 (15x10cm), white
❀ Stranded cotton - as listed in the key
❀ Tapestry needle - size 24
❀ Card - with a 4x3in (10x7,5cm) oval
  opening, Roses, Honeysuckle and
  Forget-me-nots (DMC)
❀ 2oz wadding - 4x3in (10x7.5cm)

Grandma's Bear Key

Anchor	DMC	Madeira		Colour
Cross stitch in two strands				
046	666	0210	◆◆	Red
146	798	1004	■■	Medium Blue
204	954	1211	◇◇	Light Green
352	300	2304	●●	Medium Brown
458	3325	1003	××	Light Blue
943	437	1910	□□	Light Brown

Backstitch all lines in one strand

310	403	Black		Black

Finished size: Stitch count 24 high x 19 wide
Fabric and approximate finished design area:
11 aida 2⅛ in x 1¾ in 14 aida 1¾ in x 1⅜ in
18 aida 1⅜ in x 1 in.

Teddy Bridesmaid Key

DMC	Anchor	Madeira		Colour
Cross stitch in two strands				
680	901	2210	··	Light brown
898	359	2006	■■	Dark brown
3607	087	0706	○○	Dark pink
3609	085	0709	××	Pink

Backstitch all lines in one strand

898	359	2006		Dark brown
3607	087	0706		Dark pink shoes

French Knots in one strand are worked randomly using oddments of thread for the headress and floral ring

Finished size: Stitch count 26 high x 16 wide
Fabric and approximate finished design area:
11 aida 2½ x 1⅜in 14 aida 1⅞ x 1⅛in
18 aida 1½ x ⅞in

For Panda Bear You Will Need

❀ 14HPI aida - 3½x4in (9x10cm), pale blue

❀ Stranded cotton - as listed in the key

❀ Tapestry needle - size 24

❀ Paper weight - heart-shaped, glass, Framecraft

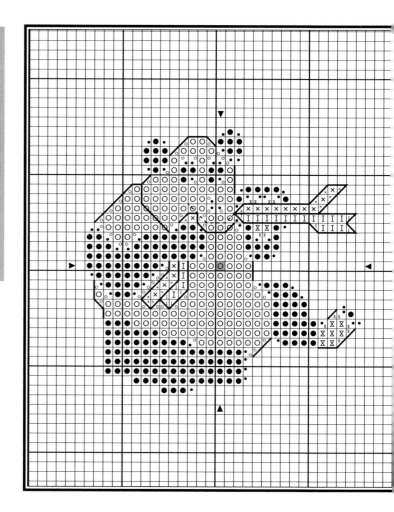

For Hammock Bear You Will Need

❀ 14HPI aida - 3x3in (7.5x7.5cm), white

❀ Stranded cotton - as listed in the key

❀ Tapestry needle - size 24

❀ Frame - 2½in, (6.5cm) round, gold effect

❀ 2oz wadding - 2½x2½in (6.5x6.5cm)

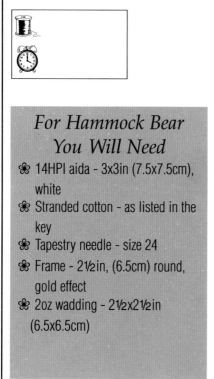

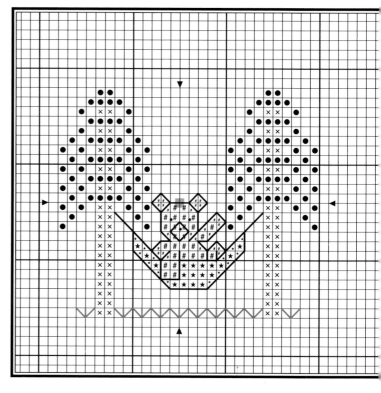

Panda Key

DMC	Anchor	Madeira		Colour
Cross stitch in two strands				
White	002	White	o o	White
310	403	Black	● ●	Black
437	362	1910	x x	Beige
3345	268	1406	× ×	Dark Green
3347	266	1408	I I	Light Green

DMC	Anchor	Madeira		Colour
Backstitch all lines in one strand				
310	403	Black		Black main outlines

DMC	Anchor	Madeira		Colour
Backstitch all lines in two strands				
310	403	Black		Black mouth

Finished size: Stitch count 28 high x 30 wide
Fabric and approximate finished design area:
11 aida 2 ½ in x 2 ¾ in 14 aida 2 in x 2 ⅛ in
18 aida 1 ½ in x 1 ⅝ in.

Teddy Sampler Key

DMC	Anchor	Madeira		Colour
Cross stitch in one strand				
611	889	2107	● ●	Gold brown
612	832	2108	× ×	Light gold brown
613	956	2109	· ·	V lt gold brown
646	8581	1811	■ ■	Dark grey
648	900	1901	♥ ♥	Light grey
676	891	2208	►◄ ►◄	Old gold
754	006	0305	# #	Light peach
926	850	1707	★ ★	Grey blue
927	848	1708	∩ ∩	Light grey blue
930	922	1712	▲ ▲	Dark blue
932	920	0710	◆ ◆	Light blue
3778	337	0402	+ +	Dark peach
3779	868	0403	⊙ ⊙	Light peach

DMC	Anchor	Madeira		Colour
Backstitch all lines in one strand				
646	8581	1811		Dark grey top line of quilt
839	380	1913		Brown bear details
930	922	1712		Dark blue inner border, lettering and bow
3778	337	0402		Dark peach outer borders and hearts

Finished size: Stitch count 110 high x 85 wide
Fabric and approximate finished design area:
14 hpi 7⅞ x 6in 18 aida 6⅛ x 4¾ in

Hammock Bear Key

Anchor	DMC	Madeira		Colour
Cross stitch in two strands				
307	783	2212	★ ★	Orange
373	422	2103	# #	Light brown
889	370	2106	× ×	Brown
924	730	1614	● ●	Dark green

Anchor	DMC	Madeira		Colour
Backstitch all lines in one strand				
203	564	1211		Light green grass
401	413	1809		Dark grey hammock and bear

Anchor	DMC	Madeira		Colour
French knots in one strand				
401	413	1809	· ·	Dark grey eyes and nose

Finished size: Stitch count 24 high x 28 wide
Fabric and approximate finished design area:
11 aida 2¼x2½in 14 aida 1¾x2in
18 aida 1⅜x1⅝in

For Teddy Sampler You Will Need

- ❀ 14HPI aida - 5x4in (12.5x10cm), white
- ❀ Stranded cotton - as listed in the key
- ❀ Tapestry needle - size 24
- ❀ Flexi-hoop - 4x3in (10x7.5cm) red, oval

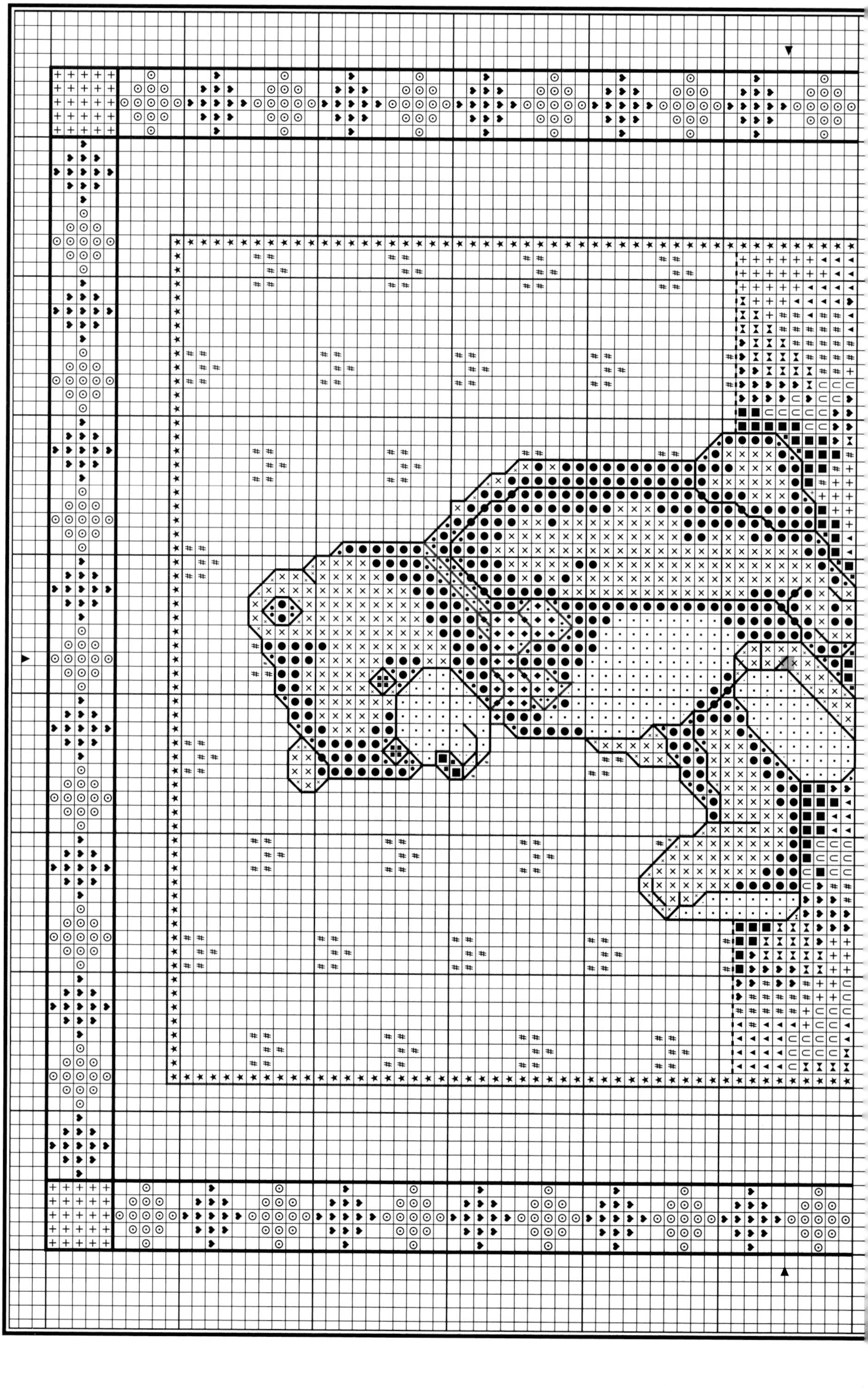

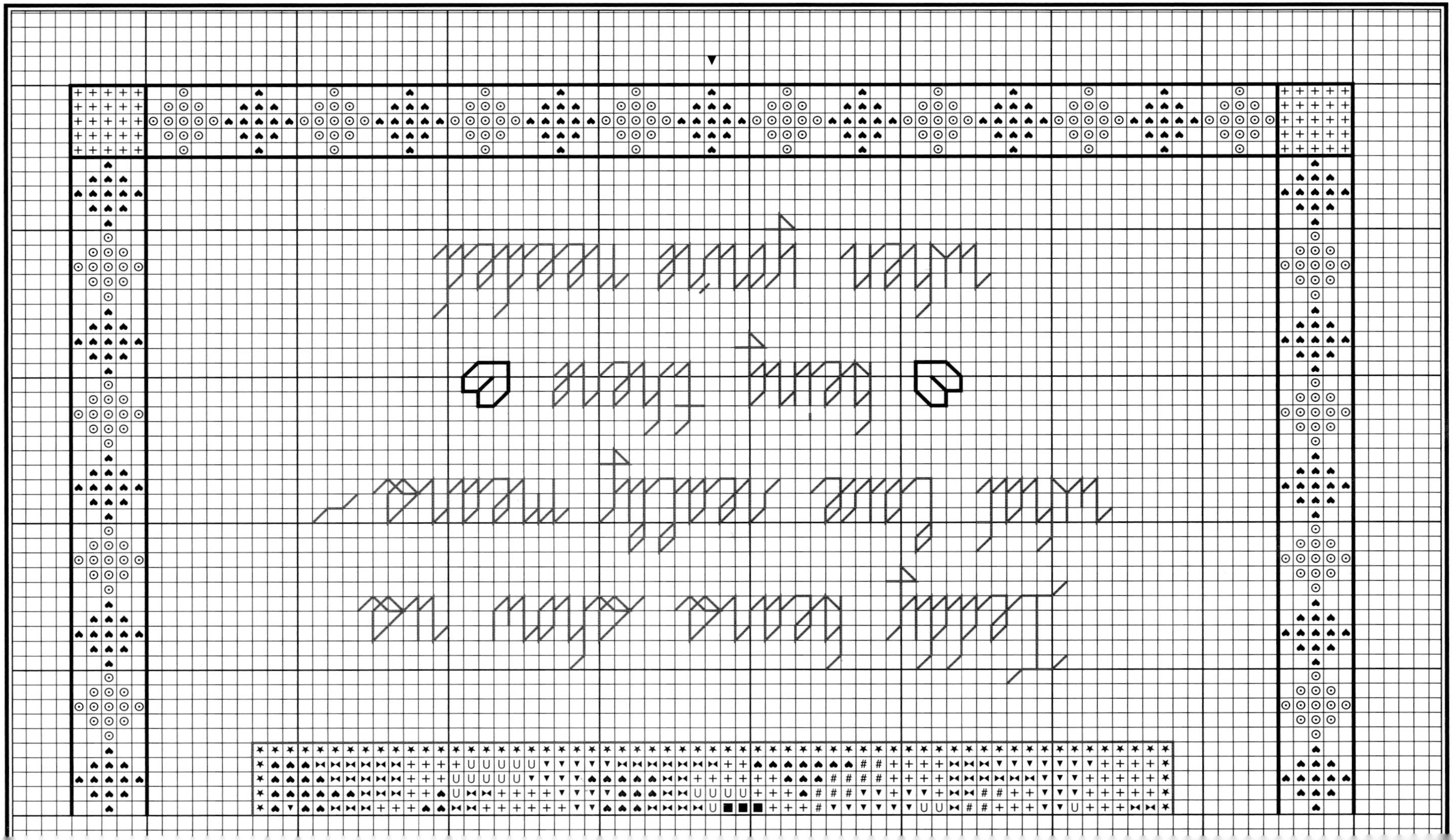

Homeward Bound

❀ ❀ ❀

There's no place quite like home, so why not stitch a piece
for your own sweet home?

Working Instructions

All the projects are worked in two strands of stranded cotton, with one strand for the backstitch. Follow the instructions on pp.15-17 for making up the projects into cards and fitting into small frames.

For the Farmhouse You will need

❀ 14HPI aida - 5x5in (12.5x12.5cm), white

❀ Stranded cotton - as listed in the key

❀ Tapestry needle - size 24

❀ Porcelain box - 4in (10cm) round, white

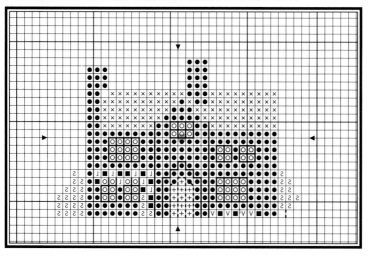

Farmhouse Key

DMC	Anchor	Madeira		Colour
Cross stitch in two strands				
White	001	White	o o	White
502	876	1703	ƨ ƨ	Medium green
640	903	1905	x x	Tawny medium
745	300	0111	v v	Light yellow
815	022	0513	■ ■	Dark burgundy
841	378	1911	+ +	Medium fawn
3033	388	1909	● ●	Light ecru
3354	074	0606	ɹ ɹ	Very light rose

Backstitch all lines in one strand

640	903	1905		Tawny medium house and window detail
3371	382	2004		Dark brown door detail

Our model was stitched using DMC threads; the Anchor and Madeira conversions are not necessarily exact colour equivalents.

Finished size: Stitch count 20 high x 32 wide
Fabric and approximate finished design area:
11HPI aida 1⅞x3in 14HPI aida 1½x2⅜in
18HPI aida 1⅛x1⅞in

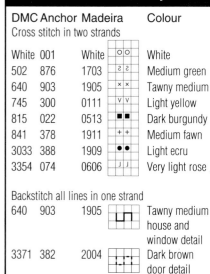

Windmill Key

DMC	Anchor	Madeira		Colour
Cross stitch in two strands				
061	1243	2212	x x	Light brown
938	380	2005	o o	Dark brown

Backstitch all lines in one strand

310	403	Black		Black windmill detail

Our model was stitched using DMC threads; the Anchor and Madeira conversions are not necessarily exact colour equivalents.

Finished size: Stitch count 24 high x 14 wide
Fabric and approximate finished design area:
11HPI aida 2¼x1¼in 14HPI aida 1¾x1in
18HPI aida 1½x⅞in

For Windmill You will need

❀ 14HPI aida - 3½x4½in (8.3x11.3cm), cream

❀ Stranded cotton - as listed in the key

❀ Tapestry needle - size 24

❀ Card - with a 2½in (6.3cm) round opening, cream

❀ 2oz wadding - 2½in (6.3cm) round

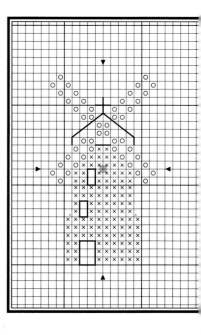

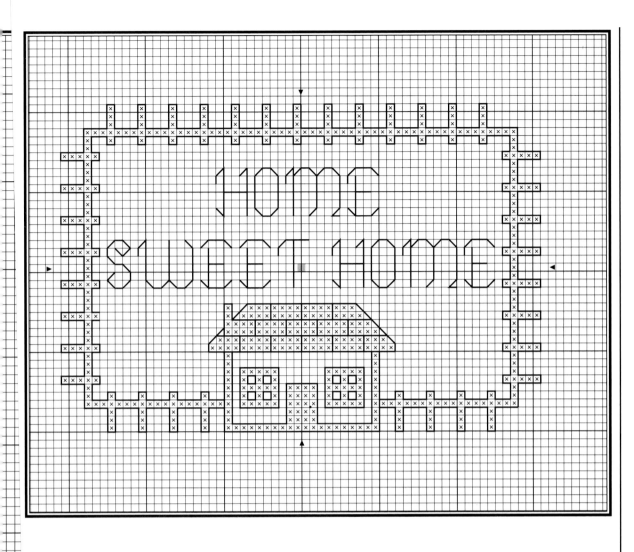

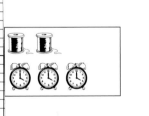

Home Sampler Key

DMC	Anchor	Madeira		Colour
Cross stitch in one strand				
676	891	2208		Dark cream
Backstitch all lines in one strand				
902	072	0601		Dark burgundy lettering and outlines
French knots in one strand				
902	072	0601		Dark burgundy door handle

Our model was stitched using DMC threads; the Anchor and Madeira conversions are not necessarily exact colour equivalents.

Finished size: Stitch count 41 high x 62 wide
Fabric and approximate finished design area:
11HPI aida 3¾x7½in 14HPI aida 3x5⅞in
18HPI aida 2⅜x4⅝in

For Home Sampler You will need

❀ 14HPI aida - 190x11in (235x27.5cm), white
❀ Stranded cotton - as listed in the key
❀ Tapestry needle - size 24
❀ Frame - 8x9in (20x22.5cm), red coloured wood with gilt trim
❀ 2oz wadding - 6½x7½in (16.3x18.8cm)

Fairy Castle Key

DMC	Anchor	Madeira		Colour
Cross stitch in two strands				
317	235	1801	××	Slate grey
436	363	2011	□□	Dark gold
451	233	1808	♦♦	Light grey
738	942	2013	2 2	Gold
746	386	0101	· ·	Cream
3778	337	2310	◎◎	Salmon

DMC	Anchor	Madeira		Colour
Backstitch all lines in one strand				
400	351	2305		Red brown Outline on salmon pink roofs
413	401	1714		Medium grey building details and windows
451	233	1808		Light grey hills behind castle
501	878	1705		Pine green trees
522	860	1602		Light green mountains

DMC	Anchor	Madeira		Colour
3799	236	1713		Dark grey Outline on grey roofs and ground in front of castle
French knots in one strand				
3799	236	1713		Dark grey tops of flag polesand portholes in gatehouse

Our model was stitched using DMC threads; the Anchor and Madeira conversions are not necessarily exact colour equivalents.

Finished size: Stitch count 52 high x 82 wide
Fabric and approximate finished design area:
11HPI aida 4 ¾ in x 7 ⅜ in 14HPI aida 3 ¾ in x 5 ⅞ in 18HPI aida 2 ⅞ in x 4 ½ in

For the Fairy Castle You will need

- ❈ 14HPI aida - 8x8in (20x20cm), white
- ❈ Stranded cotton - as listed in the key
- ❈ Tapestry needle - size 24
- ❈ Flexi-hoop - 6½in (16.3cm) round, rope, green
- ❈ Felt - 6½in (16.3cm), round, green

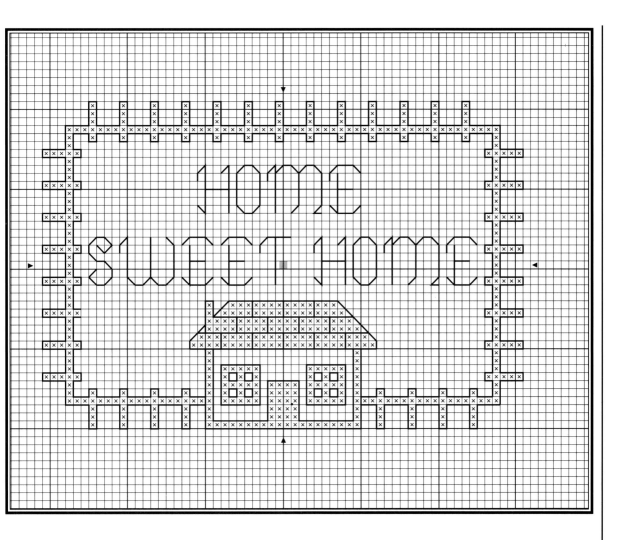

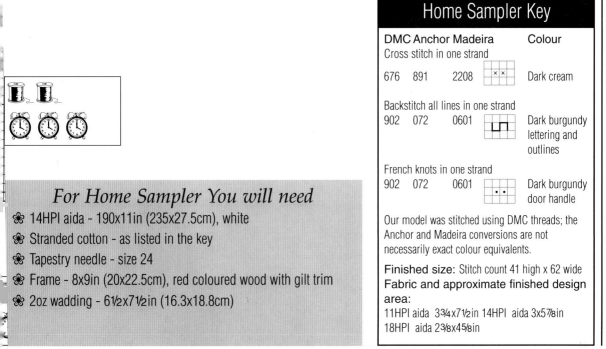

Home Sampler Key

DMC	Anchor	Madeira		Colour
Cross stitch in one strand				
676	891	2208	××	Dark cream
Backstitch all lines in one strand				
902	072	0601		Dark burgundy lettering and outlines
French knots in one strand				
902	072	0601	••	Dark burgundy door handle

Our model was stitched using DMC threads; the Anchor and Madeira conversions are not necessarily exact colour equivalents.

Finished size: Stitch count 41 high x 62 wide
Fabric and approximate finished design area:
11HPI aida 3¾x7½in 14HPI aida 3x5⅞in
18HPI aida 2⅜x4⅝in

For Home Sampler You will need

❁ 14HPI aida - 190x11in (235x27.5cm), white
❁ Stranded cotton - as listed in the key
❁ Tapestry needle - size 24
❁ Frame - 8x9in (20x22.5cm), red coloured wood with gilt trim
❁ 2oz wadding - 6½x7½in (16.3x18.8cm)

Fairy Castle Key

DMC	Anchor	Madeira		Colour
Cross stitch in two strands				
317	235	1801	××	Slate grey
436	363	2011	□□	Dark gold
451	233	1808	◆◆	Light grey
738	942	2013	2 2	Gold
746	386	0101	· ·	Cream
3778	337	2310	⊚⊚	Salmon

DMC	Anchor	Madeira		Colour
Backstitch all lines in one strand				
400	351	2305		Red brown Outline on salmon pink roofs
413	401	1714		Medium grey building details and windows
451	233	1808		Light grey hills behind castle
501	878	1705		Pine green trees
522	860	1602		Light green mountains

DMC	Anchor	Madeira		Colour
3799	236	1713		Dark grey Outline on grey roofs and ground in front of castle

French knots in one strand

DMC	Anchor	Madeira		Colour
3799	236	1713		Dark grey tops of flag poles and portholes in gatehouse

Our model was stitched using DMC threads; the Anchor and Madeira conversions are not necessarily exact colour equivalents.

Finished size: Stitch count 52 high x 82 wide **Fabric and approximate finished design area:**
11HPI aida 4 ¾ in x 7 ⅜ in 14HPI aida 3 ¾ in x 5 ⅞ in 18HPI aida 2 ⅞ in x 4 ½ in

For the Fairy Castle You will need

❀ 14HPI aida - 8x8in (20x20cm), white
❀ Stranded cotton - as listed in the key
❀ Tapestry needle - size 24
❀ Flexi-hoop - 6½in (16.3cm) round, rope, green
❀ Felt - 6½in (16.3cm) round, green

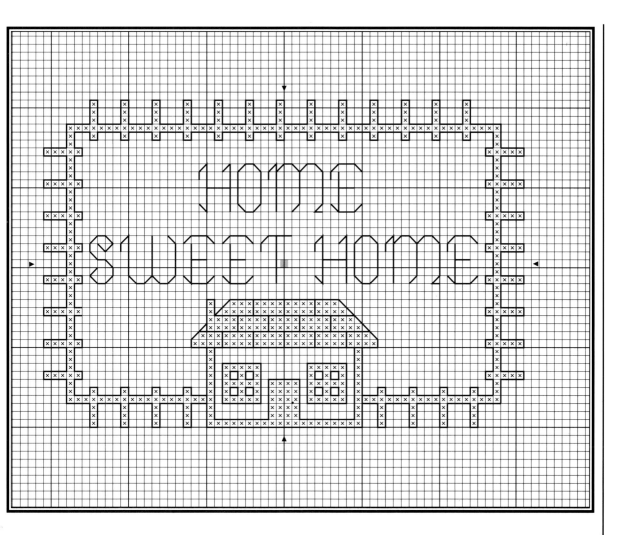

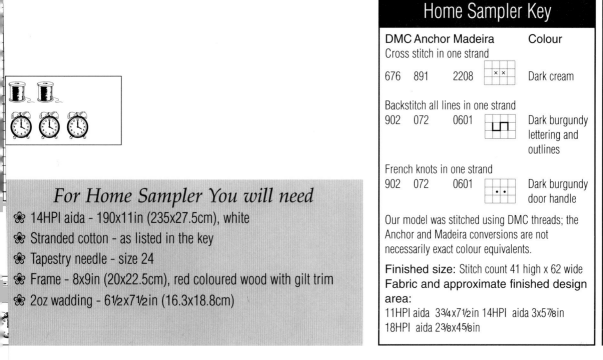

Home Sampler Key

DMC Anchor Madeira   **Colour**

Cross stitch in one strand

DMC	Anchor	Madeira		Colour
676	891	2208	××	Dark cream

Backstitch all lines in one strand

DMC	Anchor	Madeira		Colour
902	072	0601		Dark burgundy lettering and outlines

French knots in one strand

DMC	Anchor	Madeira		Colour
902	072	0601	• •	Dark burgundy door handle

Our model was stitched using DMC threads; the Anchor and Madeira conversions are not necessarily exact colour equivalents.

Finished size: Stitch count 41 high x 62 wide
Fabric and approximate finished design area:
11HPI aida 3¾x7½in 14HPI aida 3x5⅞in
18HPI aida 2⅜x4⅝in

For Home Sampler You will need

* 14HPI aida - 190x11in (235x27.5cm), white
* Stranded cotton - as listed in the key
* Tapestry needle - size 24
* Frame - 8x9in (20x22.5cm), red coloured wood with gilt trim
* 2oz wadding - 6½x7½in (16.3x18.8cm)

Fairy Castle Key

Cross stitch in two strands

DMC	Anchor	Madeira		Colour
317	235	1801	××	Slate grey
436	363	2011	□□	Dark gold
451	233	1808	◆◆	Light grey
738	942	2013	2 2	Gold
746	386	0101	· ·	Cream
3778	337	2310	⊙⊙	Salmon

Backstitch all lines in one strand

DMC	Anchor	Madeira		Colour
400	351	2305		Red brown Outline on salmon pink roofs
413	401	1714		Medium grey building details and windows
451	233	1808		Light grey hills behind castle
501	878	1705		Pine green trees
522	860	1602		Light green mountains

DMC	Anchor	Madeira		Colour
3799	236	1713		Dark grey Outline on grey roofs and ground in front of castle

French knots in one strand

DMC	Anchor	Madeira		Colour
3799	236	1713		Dark grey tops of flag poles and portholes in gatehouse

Our model was stitched using DMC threads; the Anchor and Madeira conversions are not necessarily exact colour equivalents.

Finished size: Stitch count 52 high x 82 wide
Fabric and approximate finished design area:
11HPI aida 4 ¾ in x 7 ⅜ in 14HPI aida 3 ¾ in x 5 ⅞ in 18HPI aida 2 ⅞ in x 4 ½ in

For the Fairy Castle You will need

❀ 14HPI aida - 8x8in (20x20cm), white
❀ Stranded cotton - as listed in the key
❀ Tapestry needle - size 24
❀ Flexi-hoop - 6½in (16.3cm) round, rope green
❀ Felt - 6½in (16.3cm) round, green

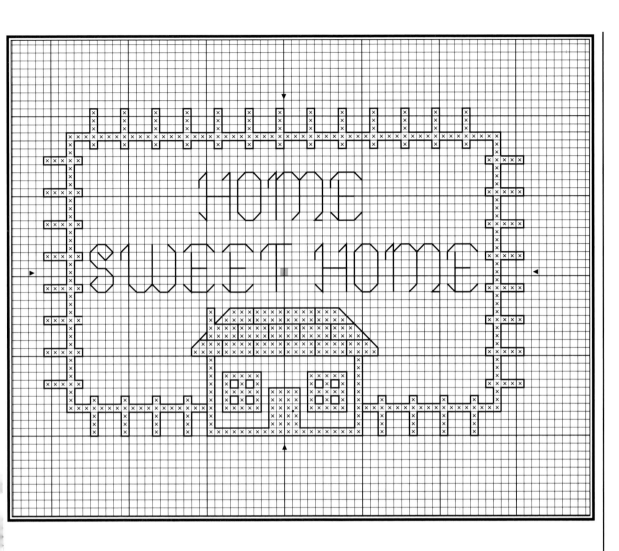

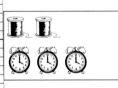

For Home Sampler You will need

❋ 14HPI aida - 190x11in (235x27.5cm), white
❋ Stranded cotton - as listed in the key
❋ Tapestry needle - size 24
❋ Frame - 8x9in (20x22.5cm), red coloured wood with gilt trim
❋ 2oz wadding - 6½x7½in (16.3x18.8cm)

Home Sampler Key

DMC	Anchor	Madeira		Colour
Cross stitch in one strand				
676	891	2208	××	Dark cream
Backstitch all lines in one strand				
902	072	0601	⌐⌐	Dark burgundy lettering and outlines
French knots in one strand				
902	072	0601	• •	Dark burgundy door handle

Our model was stitched using DMC threads; the Anchor and Madeira conversions are not necessarily exact colour equivalents.

Finished size: Stitch count 41 high x 62 wide
Fabric and approximate finished design area:
11HPI aida 3¾x7½in 14HPI aida 3x5⅞in
18HPI aida 2⅜x4⅝in

Fairy Castle Key

DMC	Anchor	Madeira		Colour
Cross stitch in two strands				
317	235	1801	× ×	Slate grey
436	363	2011	□ □	Dark gold
451	233	1808	◆ ◆	Light grey
738	942	2013	2 2	Gold
746	386	0101	· ·	Cream
3778	337	2310	⊙ ⊙	Salmon
Backstitch all lines in one strand				
400	351	2305		Red brown Outline on salmon pink roofs
413	401	1714		Medium grey building details and windows
451	233	1808		Light grey hills behind castle
501	878	1705		Pine green trees
522	860	1602		Light green mountains

DMC	Anchor	Madeira		Colour
3799	236	1713		Dark grey Outline on grey roofs and ground in front of castle
French knots in one strand				
3799	236	1713	· ·	Dark grey tops of flag polesand portholes in gatehouse

Our model was stitched using DMC threads; the Anchor and Madeira conversions are not necessarily exact colour equivalents.

Finished size: Stitch count 52 high x 82 wide Fabric and approximate finished design area:
11HPI aida 4 ¾ in x 7 ⅜ in 14HPI aida 3 ¾ in x 5 ⅞ in 18HPI aida 2 ⅞ in x 4 ½ in

For the Fairy Castle You will need

❀ 14HPI aida - 8x8in (20x20cm), white
❀ Stranded cotton - as listed in the key
❀ Tapestry needle - size 24
❀ Flexi-hoop - 6½in (16.3cm) round, rope, green
❀ Felt - 6½in (16.3cm), round, green

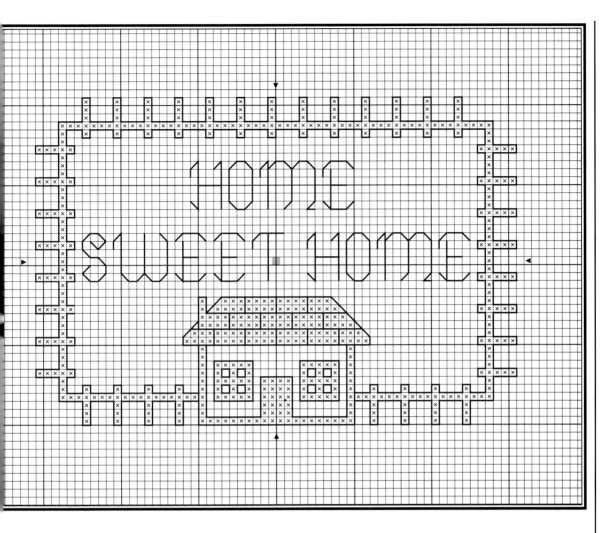

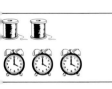

For Home Sampler You will need

- 14HPI aida - 190x11in (235x27.5cm), white
- Stranded cotton - as listed in the key
- Tapestry needle - size 24
- Frame - 8x9in (20x22.5cm), red coloured wood with gilt trim
- 2oz wadding - 6½x7½in (16.3x18.8cm)

Home Sampler Key

DMC	Anchor	Madeira		Colour
Cross stitch in one strand				
676	891	2208		Dark cream
Backstitch all lines in one strand				
902	072	0601		Dark burgundy lettering and outlines
French knots in one strand				
902	072	0601		Dark burgundy door handle

Our model was stitched using DMC threads; the Anchor and Madeira conversions are not necessarily exact colour equivalents.

**Finished size: Stitch count 41 high x 62 wide
Fabric and approximate finished design area:**
11HPI aida 3¾x7½in 14HPI aida 3x5⅞in
18HPI aida 2⅜x4⅝in

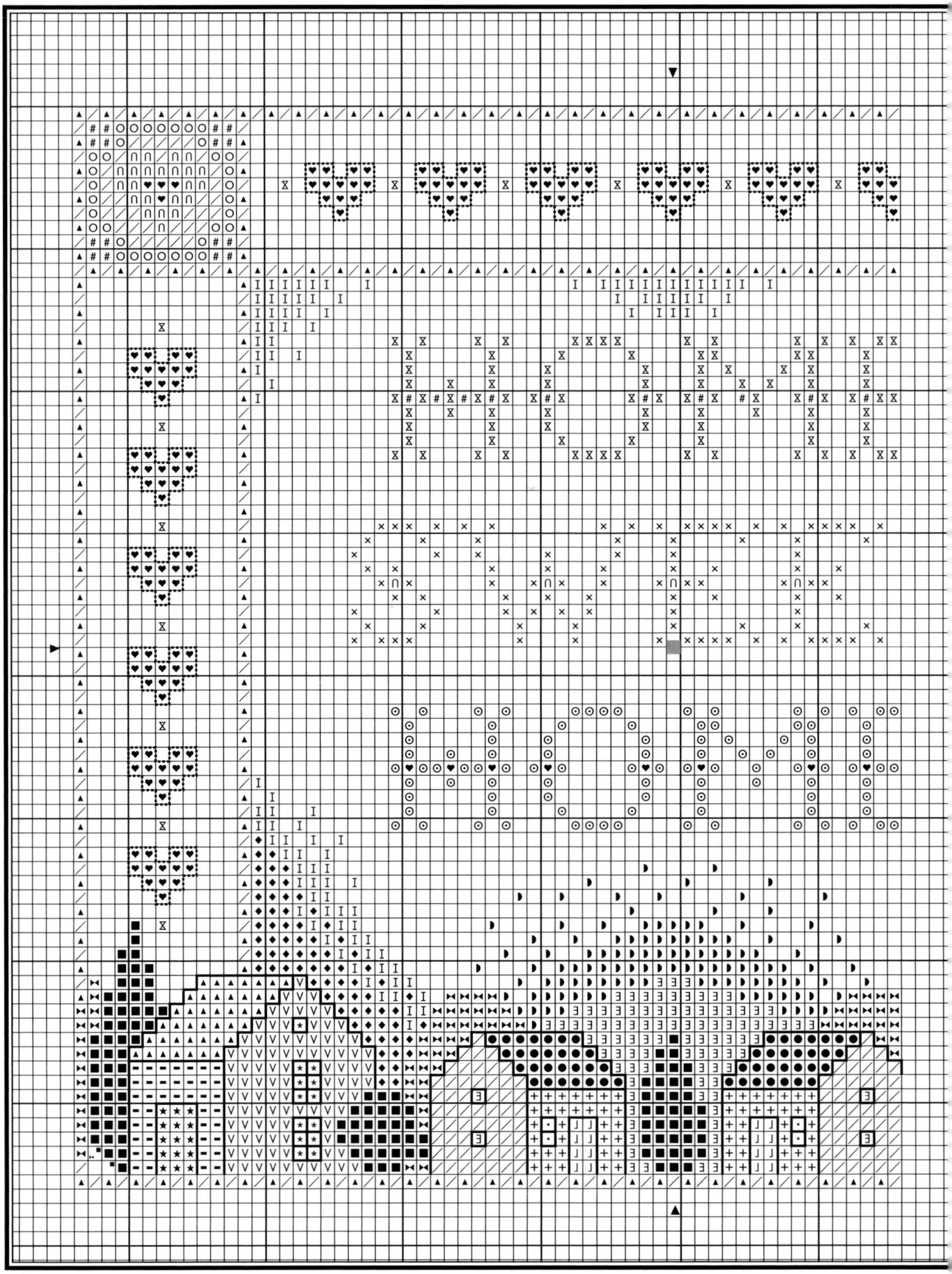

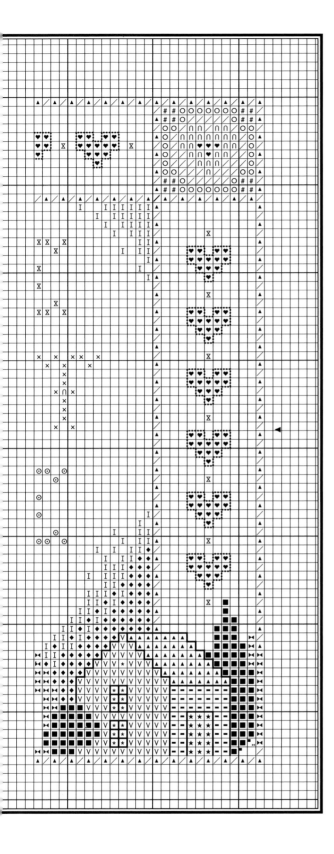

Home Sweet Home Key

DMC Anchor Madeira   **Colour**

Cross stitch in two strands

DMC	Anchor	Madeira			Colour
221	020	0513	J	J	Dark red
340	118	0902	★	★	Lilac
351	011	0214	#	#	Apricot
352	010	0406	∩	∩	Dark peach
353	009	0405	♥	♥	Light peach
400	351	2305	▲	▲	Dark brown
407	347	2301	-	-	Light brown
434	309	2009	●	●	Brown
727	293	0110	▶	▶	Light yellow
743	302	0114	℈	℈	Yellow
797	132	0912	*	*	Royal blue
798	131	0911	·	·	Blue
827	159	1014	◆	◆	Light blue
828	158	1101	I	I	Very light blue
950	881	2309	+	+	Beige
987	244	1403	⋈	⋈	Green
989	242	1401	■	■	Light green
3011	845	1608	X	X	Dark olivegreen
3012	844	1612	×	×	Medium olive green
3013	843	1605	⊙	⊙	Light olive green
3041	871	0806	○	○	Mauve
3042	869	0807	/	/	Light mauve
3774	778	1910	V	V	Light beige

Backstitch all lines in one strand

351	011	0214		Apricot outline hearts
898	359	2006		Very dark brown house outlines

Our model was stitched using DMC threads; the Anchor and Madeira conversions are not necessarily exact colour equivalents.

Finished size: Stitch count 76 high x 87 wide
Fabric and approximate finished design area:
11HPI aida 7x8in 14HPI aida 5½x6⅛in
18HPI aida 4¼x4⅞in

For Home Sweet Home You will need

❀ 18HPI aida - 6½x7½in (16.3x18.8cm), beige
❀ Stranded cotton - as listed in the key
❀ Tapestry needle - size 24
❀ Frame - 4¾x5¾in (11.9x14.4cm), wodden with gilt trim
❀ 2oz wadding - 3¾x4¾in (9.4x11.9cm)

Fairy Castle Key

DMC	Anchor	Madeira		Colour
Cross stitch in two strands				
317	235	1801	× ×	Slate grey
436	363	2011	□ □	Dark gold
451	233	1808	◆ •	Light grey
738	942	2013	2 2	Gold
746	386	0101	· ·	Cream
3778	337	2310	⊙ ⊙	Salmon

DMC	Anchor	Madeira		Colour
Backstitch all lines in one strand				
400	351	2305		Red brown Outline on salmon pink roofs
413	401	1714		Medium grey building details and windows
451	233	1808		Light grey hills behind castle
501	878	1705		Pine green trees
522	860	1602		Light green mountains

DMC	Anchor	Madeira		Colour
3799	236	1713		Dark grey Outline on grey roofs and ground in front of castle

French knots in one strand

DMC	Anchor	Madeira		Colour
3799	236	1713	· ·	Dark grey tops of flag poles and portholes in gatehouse

Our model was stitched using DMC threads; the Anchor and Madeira conversions are not necessarily exact colour equivalents.

Finished size: Stitch count 52 high x 82 wide
Fabric and approximate finished design area:
11HPI aida 4 ¾ in x 7 ⅜ in 14HPI aida 3 ¾ in x 5 ⅞ in 18HPI aida 2 ⅞ in x 4 ½ in

For the Fairy Castle You will need

- ❀ 14HPI aida - 8x8in (20x20cm), white
- ❀ Stranded cotton - as listed in the key
- ❀ Tapestry needle - size 24
- ❀ Flexi-hoop - 6½in (16.3cm) round, rope, green
- ❀ Felt - 6½in (16.3cm), round, green

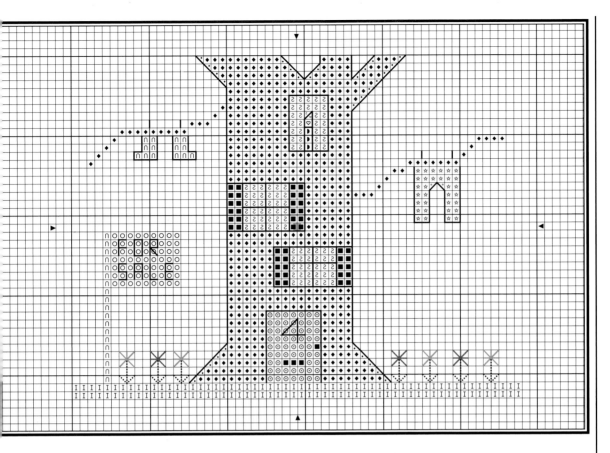

Treehouse Key

DMC	Anchor	Madeira		Colour
Cross stitch in two strands				
Ecru	387	Ecru	s s	Ecru
221	897	0811	■ ■	Cherry red
444	291	0106	n n	Yellow
666	046	0210	▸ ▸	Red
676	0891	2208	o o	Ochre
741	304	0201	▽ ▽	Orange
798	131	0911	⊙ ⊙	Sky blue
801	357	2007	# #	Dark brown
826	929	1012	☆ ☆	Cornflower blue
869	944	2106	◆ ◆	Brown green
988	243	1402	I I	Grass green

DMC	Anchor	Madeira		Colour
3371	382	2004		Very dark brown window details and lettering

Backstitch all lines in two strands

444	291	0106		Yellow flowers
666	046	0210		Red flowers

Our model was stitched using DMC threads; the Anchor and Madeira conversions are not necessarily exact colour equivalents.

Finished size: Stitch count 43 high x 58 wide
Fabric and approximate finished design area:
11HPI aida 3 ⅞ in x 5 ¼ in 14HPI aida 3 in x 4 ⅛ in
18HPI aida 2 ⅜ in x 3 ¼ in

Backstitch all lines in one strand

319	246	1405		Dark green flower stems

For the Treehouse You will need

❀ 14HPI aida - 5x7in (12.5x17.5cm), white
❀ Stranded cotton - as listed in the key
❀ Tapestry needle - size 24
❀ Child's dungarees
❀ Sewing kit - needle, thread, pins

Junior Gymkhana

❁ ❁ ❁

*Who can resist the thrills of a gymkhana? Make one of these
figures for a card or put them all together as a fun picture.*

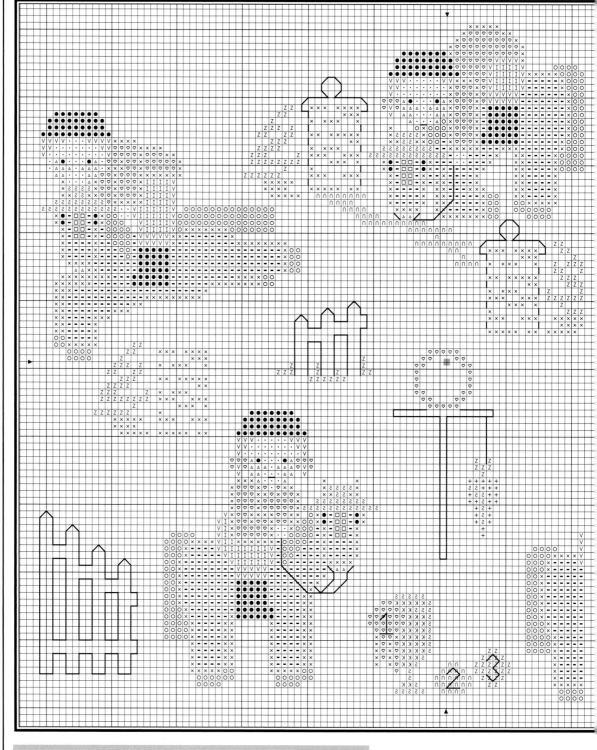

For Junior Gymkhana You will Need

- ❀ 14HPI aida - 13x15in (32.5x37.5cm), white
- ❀ Stranded cotton - as listed in the key
- ❀ Tapestry needle
- ❀ Wooden frame - 10x12in (25x30cm), blue
- ❀ Mount - with a 7½inx9½in (18.75x23.75cm) rectangle cut from the centre, blue

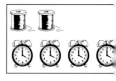

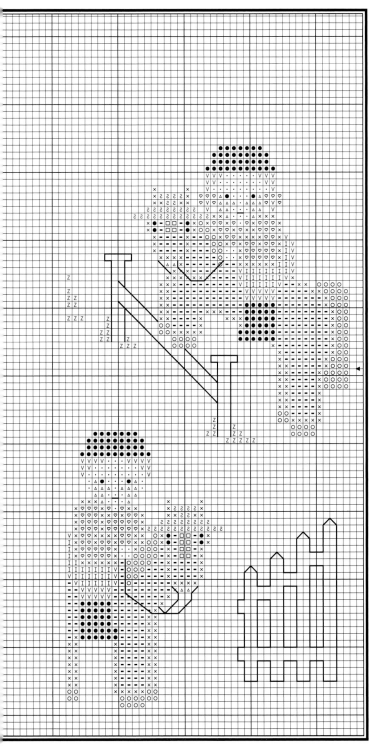

Junior Gymkhana Key

Anchor	DMC	Madeira		Colour
Cross stitch in two strands				
001	White	White	□ □	White
006	754	0305	· ·	Light pink
008	353	0304	▵ ▵	Pink
144	800	1014	⌐ ⌐	Blue
229	700	1304	z z	Green
301	744	0110	⋋ ⋋	Yellow
303	742	0114	ƨ ƨ	Gold
316	740	0203	+ +	Orange
335	606	0209	♡ ♡	Red
341	919	0313	× ×	Rust
378	841	1911	v v	Fawn
380	839	1913	○ ○	Brown
388	3033	1909	I I	Light fawn
403	310	Black	● ●	Black
883	3064	2312	– –	Light brown

| Backstitch in one strand | | | | |
| 403 | 310 | Black | | Black outlines and details |

Our model was stitched using Anchor threads; the DMC and Madeira conversions are not necessarily exact colour equivalents.

Finished size: Stitch count 100 high x 126 wide
Fabric and approximate finished design area:
11HPI aida 9x11½ins
14HPI aida7⅛x9ins
18HPI aida5½x7ins

Working Instructions

The cross stitch is worked in two strands of stranded cotton.

Work the back stitch in one strand of black for the reins, fences, numbers and outline on the walls.

Each pony and rider can be worked as an individual picture. If you have a particular horse-riding friend you could change the colour of the jacket or the rider's hair to match their own.

The Land of Childhood Dreams

Babies are one of life's greatest gifts. Why not stitch a special baby gift that will be enjoyed in childhood and treasured in later life?

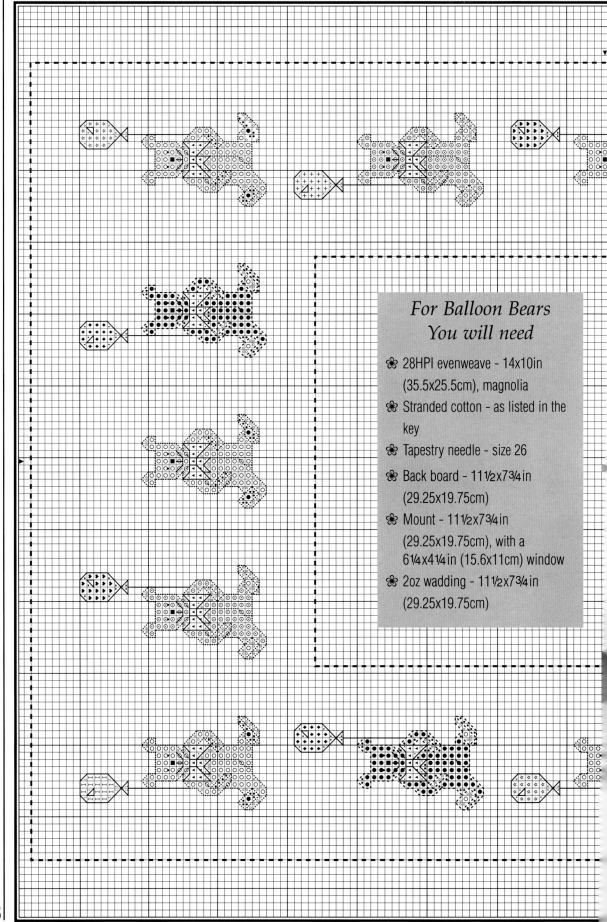

For Balloon Bears
You will need

❀ 28HPI evenweave - 14x10in (35.5x25.5cm), magnolia
❀ Stranded cotton - as listed in the key
❀ Tapestry needle - size 26
❀ Back board - 11½x7¾in (29.25x19.75cm)
❀ Mount - 11½x7¾in (29.25x19.75cm), with a 6¼x4¼in (15.6x11cm) window
❀ 2oz wadding - 11½x7¾in (29.25x19.75cm)

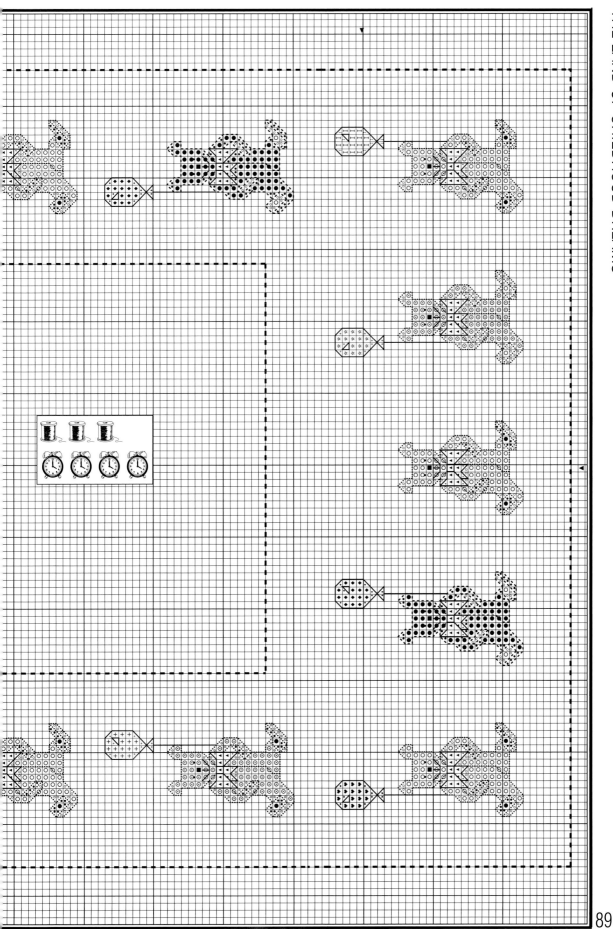

Balloon Bears Key

DMC	Anchor	Madeira		Colour
Cross stitch in two strands				
310	403	Black	■ ■	Black
420	375	2105	⊙ ⊙	Medium Brown
422	373	2103	○ ○	Light Brown
721	324	0309	▲ ▲	Orange
727	293	0110	I I	Yellow
817	9046	0211	◆ ◆	Red
826	161	1012	♥ ♥	Dark Blue
827	159	1014	☆ ☆	Light Blue
869	944	2105	● ●	Dark Brown
3348	265	1209	+ +	Light Green

Backstitch all lines in one strand				
310	403	Black		Black Outline of balloons
839	380	1913		Very Dark Brown Outline of dark brown bears
869	944	2105		Dark Brown Outline of light brown and medium brown bears

French Knots				
310	403	Black		Black Eyes

Denotes border of design

Our model was stitched using DMC threads; the Anchor and Madeira conversions are not necessarily exact colour equivalents.
Finished size: Stitch count 165 high x 111 wide
Fabric and approximate finished design area:
11HPI aida 15 in x 10 in 14HPI aida 11 ¾ in x 8 in
18HPI aida 9 ⅛ in x 6 ⅛ in

Note: If you intend to make the balloon bears into a picture frame your stitches should be positioned centrally on the material size listed in the You Will Need key on page 88.

To make up the picture frame, please refer to the instructions on page 17.

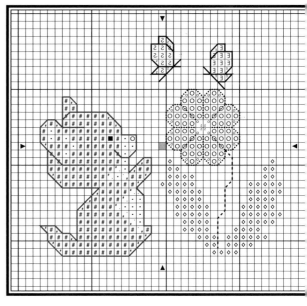

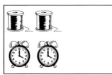

For Bear and Butterflies You will need

- ❀ 14HPI aida - 6xc4in (15x10cm), cream
- ❀ Stranded cotton - as listed in the key
- ❀ Tapestry needle - size 24
- ❀ Card - with a 3¼in (8cm) round opening, Apple Blossom (DMC)
- ❀ 2oz wadding - 3¼in (8cm) round

Bear & Butterflies Key

Anchor	DMC	Madeira		Colour
Cross stitch in two strands				
8	353	0304	○ ○	Pink
121	793	0905	Ǝ Ǝ	Blue
216	502	1513	◇ ◇	Green
275	746	0101	· ·	Cream
293	727	0110	s s	Yellow
374	3045	2104	# #	Brown
403	310	Black	■ ■	Black

Backstitch all lines in one strand				
10	352	0406		Dark Pink Outline of Flower
216	502	1513		Green Flower Stem
403	310	Black		Black Outline of butterflies
944	869	2106		Dark Brown Outline of bear

Our model was stitched using Anchor threads; the DMC and Madeira conversions are not necessarily exact colour equivalents.

Finished size: Stitch count 29 high x 33 wide
Fabric and approximate finished design area:
11HPI aida 2 ⅝ in x 3 in 14HPI aida 2 in x 2 ⅜ in
18HPI aida 1 ⅝ in x 1 ⅞ in

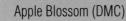

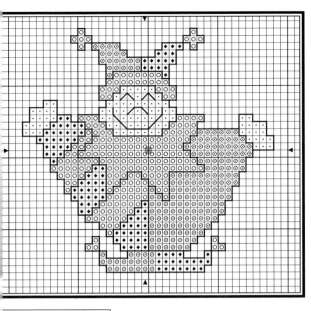

Joker Key

Anchor	DMC	Madeira		Colour
Cross stitch in two strands				
002	White	White	· ·	White
046	666	0210	♦ ♦	Red
118	340	0902	◎ ◎	Lilac
305	743	0113	○ ○	Yellow
Backstitch all lines in one strand				
403	310	Black		Black

Our model was stitched using Anchor threads; the DMC and Madeira conversions are not necessarily exact colour equivalents.

Finished size: Stitch count 34 high x 36 wide
Fabric and approximate finished design area:
11HPI aida 3 in x 3 ¼ in 14HPI aida 2 ⅜ in x 2 ½ in 18HPI aida 1 ⅞ in x 2 in

Zoo Animals Key

DMC	Anchor	Madeira		Colour
Cross stitch in two strands				
002	White	White	· ·	White
238	703	1307	▲ ▲	Green
303	742	0114	♦ ♦	Golden Brown
313	977	2301	○ ○	Orange
371	433	2008	● ●	Brown
398	415	1803	◇ ◇	Light Grey
399	318	180	# #	Medium Grey
400	317	1714	♥ ♥	Dark Grey
403	310	Black	■ ■	Black
Backstitch all lines in one strand				
303	742	0114		Golden Brown
400	317	1714		Dark Grey
403	310	Black		Black
French Knots				
303	742	0114	· ·	Golden Brown Giraffe's Horns
403	310	Black	· ·	Black Pandas Eyes

Our model was stitched using Anchor threads; the DMC and Madeira conversions are not necessarily exact colour equivalents.

Finished size: Stitch count 30 high x 28 wide
Fabric and approximate finished design area:
11HPI aida 2 ¾ in x 2 ½ in 14HPI aida 2 ⅛ in x 2 in 18HPI aida 1 ⅝ in x 1 ½ in

Zoo animals You will need

❊ 14HPI aida - 4x4in (10x10cm), cream
❊ Stranded cotton - as listed in the key
❊ Tapestry needle - size 24
❊ Porcelain box - 3in (7.5cm) round, pale blue (Framecraft)
❊ 2oz wadding - 3x3in (7.5x7.5cm) round

Joker You will need

❊ 14HPI aida - 5½x5½in (14x14cm), cream
❊ Stranded cotton - as listed in the key
❊ Tapestry needle - size 24
❊ Flexi-hoop - 4½in (11.5cm), oval, blue
❊ Felt - 4½in (11.5cm), oval, blue

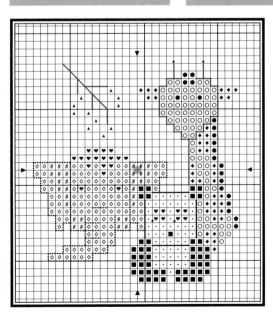

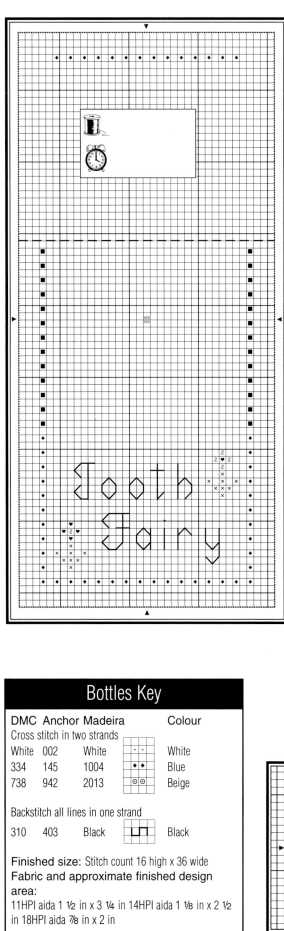

Tooth Fairy You will need

❀ 14HPI aida - 6x2¾in (15x7cm), light blue or pink

❀ Stranded cotton - as listed in the key

❀ Tapestry needle - size 24

❀ Felt - 1½x2¼in (3.8x5.7cm), light blue or pink

Tooth Fairy Key

DMC	Anchor	Madeira		Colour
Cross stitch in two strands				
47	266	408	× ×	Green
666	046	020	♥ ♥	Red
799	30	004	♦ ♦	Blue
972	298	007	₴ ₴	Yellow
799	30	004	■■ ■	Blue (2 layers)
Backstitch all lines in one strand				
799	30	04	⌐┐	Blue lettering
French knot				
799	30	004	• •	Blue dot on "i"
Denotes edge of pouch			⌐¦	
Denotes fold			⌐¦⌐	

Finished size; Stitch count 74 high x 3 wide
Fabric and approximate finished design area;
11HPI aida 6¾ x 2⅛ in (16.9 x 5cm) 14HPI aida 5¼ x 2¼in (13.2 x 5.7cm) 18HPI aida 4⅛ x 1¾ in (10.3 x 4.5 cm)

For Bottles You will need

❀ 18HPI aida - 5x5in (12.5x12.5cm), white

❀ Stranded cotton - as listed in the key

❀ Tapestry needle - size 26

❀ Flexi-hoop - 3½in (9cm) round rope, pale blue

❀ Felt - 3½in (9cm) round, pale blue

Bottles Key

DMC	Anchor	Madeira		Colour
Cross stitch in two strands				
White	002	White	· ·	White
334	145	1004	♦ ♦	Blue
738	942	2013	⊙ ⊙	Beige
Backstitch all lines in one strand				
310	403	Black	⌐┐	Black

Finished size: Stitch count 16 high x 36 wide
Fabric and approximate finished design area:
11HPI aida 1 ½ in x 3 ¼ in 14HPI aida 1 ⅛ in x 2 ½ in 18HPI aida ⅞ in x 2 in

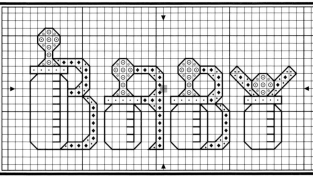

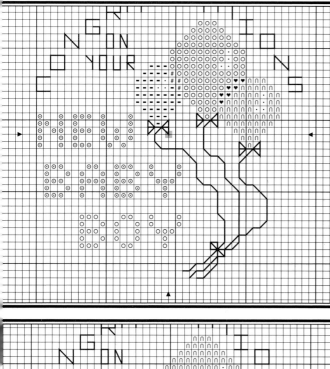

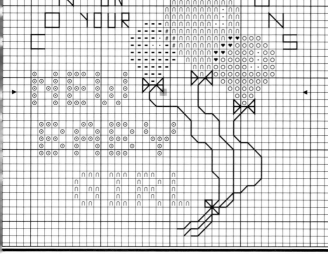

New Baby Girl Key

DMC	Anchor	Madeira		Colour
Cross stitch in two strands				
White	002	White	· ·	White
437	362	2012	○ ○	Gold
444	291	0106	- -	Yellow
776	024	0503	n n	Pink
0827	159	1014	○ ○	Blue

DMC	Anchor	Madeira		Colour
Cross stitch blending one strand of each colour				
444	291	0106	# #	Yellow
776	024	0503		Pink
776	024	0503	♥ ♥	Pink
827	159	1014		Blue

DMC	Anchor	Madeira		Colour
Backstitch all lines in one strand				
414	399	1801	⌐┌	Grey

Our model was stitched using DMC threads; the Anchor and Madeira conversions are not necessarily exact colour equivalents.

Finished size: Stitch count 40 high x 38 wide
Fabric and approximate finished design area:
11HPI aida 3 5/8 in x 3 1/2 in 14HPI aida 2 7/8 in x 2 3/4 in 18HPI aida 2 1/4 in x 2 1/8 in

New Baby Boy Key

DMC	Anchor	Madeira		Colour
Cross stitch in two strands				
White	002	White	· ·	White
444	291	0106	- -	Yellow
776	024	0503	n n	Pink
0827	159	1014	○ ○	Blue

DMC	Anchor	Madeira		Colour
Cross stitch blending one strand of each colour				
444	291	0106	# #	Yellow
827	159	1014		Blue
776	024	0503	♥ ♥	Pink
827	159	1014		Blue
437	362	2012		Gold
827	159	1014	○ ○	Blue

DMC	Anchor	Madeira		Colour
Backstitch all lines in one strand				
414	399	1801	⌐┌	Grey

Our model was stitched using DMC threads; the Anchor and Madeira conversions are not necessarily exact colour equivalents.

Finished size: Stitch count 40 high x 38 wide
Fabric and approximate finished design area:
11HPI aida 3 5/8 in x 3 1/2 in 14HPI aida 2 7/8 in x 2 3/4 in 18HPI aida 2 1/4 in x 2 1/8 in

New Baby Girl/Boy
You will need

- ❊ 14HPI aida - 5x5in (12.5x12.5cm), cream
- ❊ Stranded cotton - as listed in the key
- ❊ Tapestry needle - size 24
- ❊ Frame - 4x4in, (10x10cm), white with gold or silver edge
- ❊ 2oz wadding - 3 1/4 x 3 1/4 in (8x8cm)

Perfect Timing

❀ ❀ ❀

Take time to stitch one of our country clock faces to
adorn your mantelpiece.

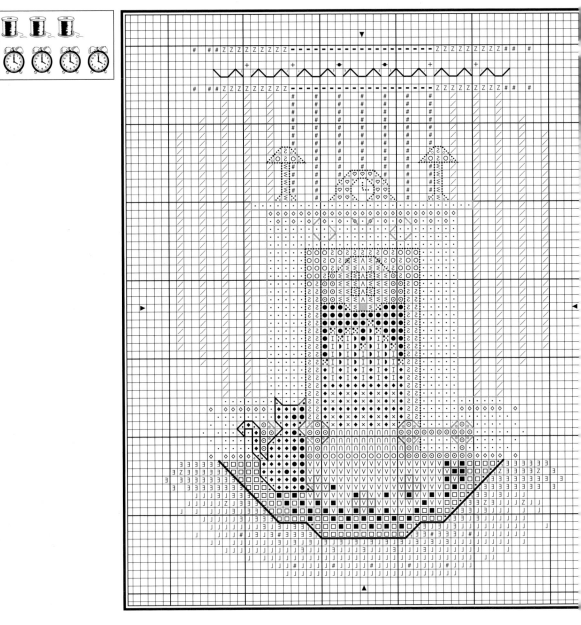

For Clock on Mantelpiece You will Need

- ❀ 22HPI evenweave fabric - 11x9in (28x23cm), white
- ❀ Stranded cotton - as listed in the key
- ❀ Tapestry needle - size 24
- ❀ Frame - 9½x8in (24.5x20.5cm), dark wood
- ❀ Mount - with a 6½x5in (16.5x12.5cm) rectangular opening
- ❀ 2oz wadding - 6½x5in (16.5x12.5cm)

How to work the main fireplace design

The cross stitch is worked in three strands of cotton over two threads of fabric.

Work the back stitch in one strand of thread in the colours listed in the key.

How to Make the Fringe

Work each of the tassels on the edge of the rug separately.

Starting at the outside corner of the rug, take the needle and thread from the front to the back of your stitching, leaving a 1in (2.5cm) tail of stranded cotton on the right side.

Bring the needle back to the front of your work alongside the tail and tie a knot.

Pass the needle to the back of the work before securing the thread. The carpet fringe can then be trimmed to the length required.

Clock On Mantle Shelf Key

DMC	Anchor	Madeira		Colour
Cross stitch in three strands				
White	002	White	· ·	White
Ecru	387	Ecru	v v	Ecru
221	020	0811	‒ ‒	Burgundy
223	894	0813	z z	Medium Light Pink
224	893	0812	# #	Light Pink
225	892	0501	/ /	Very light Pink
368	215	1310	з з	Light Green
369	202	1309	j j	Mint Green
369	268	1504	o o	Dark Green
370	266	1502	s s	Green
371	266	1408	n n	Avocado Green
646	8581	1811	● ●	Medium Grey
677	886	2205	^ ^	Cream
722	323	0307	▸ ▸	Light Orange
738	361	2012	□ □	Light Brown
739	885	1909	■ ■	Sandstone Light
742	303	0114	I I	Citrus Orange
793	121	0906	◆ ◆	Medium Blue
794	120	0909	+ +	Light Blue
832	907	2202	⊙ ⊙	Dark Orange
833	907	1610	≤ ≤	Brown Green
844	401	1809	♦ ♦	Very Dark Grey
869	944	2106	♥ ♥	Olive
970	324	0204	× ×	Orange
3072	847	1709	◇ ◇	Grey Mist

DMC	Anchor	Madeira		Colour
Backstitch all lines in one strand				
221	020	0811		Burgundy Crosses on rug
310	403	Black		Black Back of cat
646	8581	1811		Medium Grey Details and outline on mantlepiece and skirting board & parts of fender
869	944	2106		Olive Outline on lamps and clock and interior of fire place
970	324	0204		Orange Front of cat and glow on fender

Line for attatching tassels - see instructions

Tassels positioning

Finished size: Stitch count 68 high x 53 wide
Fabric and approximate finished design area:
11 aida 6 1/8 in. x 4 7/8 in.
14 aida 4 7/8 in. x 3 3/4 in.
18 aida 3 3/4 in. x 2 7/8 in.

For Wake Up You will need

❀ 14HPI aida - 9x9in (23x23cm)
❀ Stranded cotton - as listed in the key
❀ Tapestry needle - size 24
❀ Frame - 8x8in (20.5x20.5cm), red
❀ Mount Board - with a 6in (15cm) circular opening, yellow

Wake Up Call Key

DMC	Anchor	Madeira		Colour
Cross stitch in two strands				
310	403	Black	● ●	Black
666	046	0210	◇ ◇	Red
725	306	0113	× ×	Yellow
754	006	0305	♥ ♥	Flesh
943	188	1203	v v	Green
Backstitch all lines in one strand				
310	403	Black		Black Eyelashes
Backstitch all lines in two strands				
310	403	Black		Black Eyes

DMC	Anchor	Madeira		Colour
550	102	0714		Dark Purple Laces & Numerals
666	046	0210		Red Mouth

Finished size: Stitch count 76 high x 74 wide
Fabric and approximate finished design area:
11 aida 6 7/8 in. x 6 3/4 in.
14 aida 5 3/8 in. x 5 1/4 in.
18 aida 4 1/4 in. x 4 1/8 in.

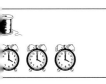

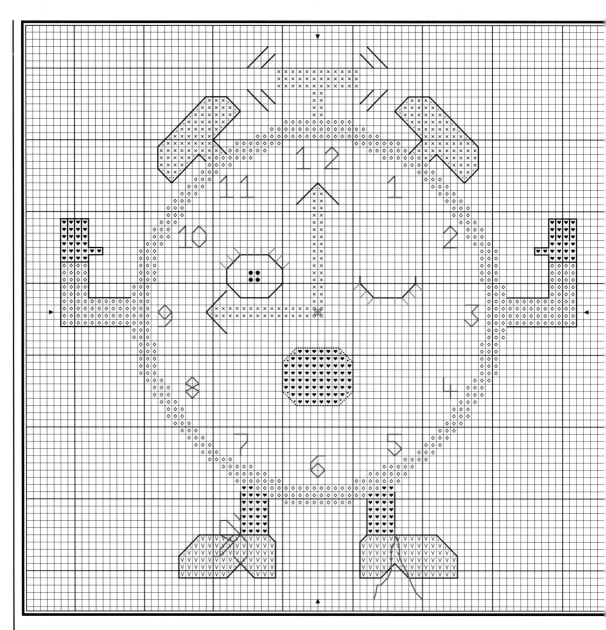

Our Family Clock Key

DMC	Anchor	Madeira		Colour
Cross stitch in two strands				
307	289	0104	⊙⊙	Bright yellow
433	371	2008	■■	Dark brown
435	369	2010	▲▲	Brown
726	297	0109	··	Dull yellow
800	136	0910	₂₂	Blue
890	218	1314	##	Dark green
3341	328	0303	♥♥	Peach
Backstitch all lines in one strand				
435	369	2010		Brown outline detail on clock

DMC	Anchor	Madeira		Colour
433	371	2008		Dark brown numerals and hands
726	297	0109		Dull yellow clock details
996	433	1103		Bright blue wallpaper stripe
French knots in one strand				
433	371	2008	··	Dark brown centre of clockface

Finished size: Stitch count 80 high x 60 wide
Fabric and approximate finished design area:
11 aida 7¼x5⅜in 14 aida 5⅝x4¼in 18 aida 4⅜x3¼in

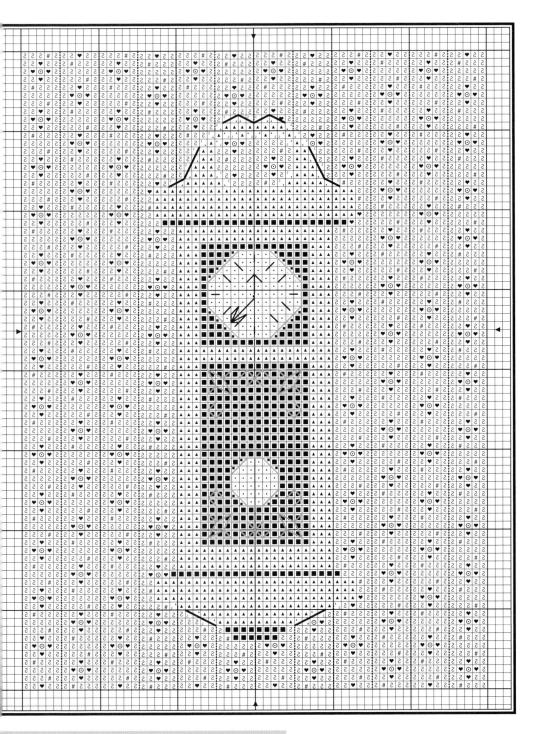

For Family Clock You will need

❀ 18HPI aida - 7x6in (18x15cm), white

❀ Stranded cotton - as listed in the key

❀ Tapestry needle - size 26

❀ Frame - 6¾x5¾in (16.75x14.5cm), dark wood

❀ Mount - with a 4⅜x3¼in (11x8cm) rectangular
   opening, blue and brown

❀ 2oz wadding - 4⅜x3¼in (11x8cm)

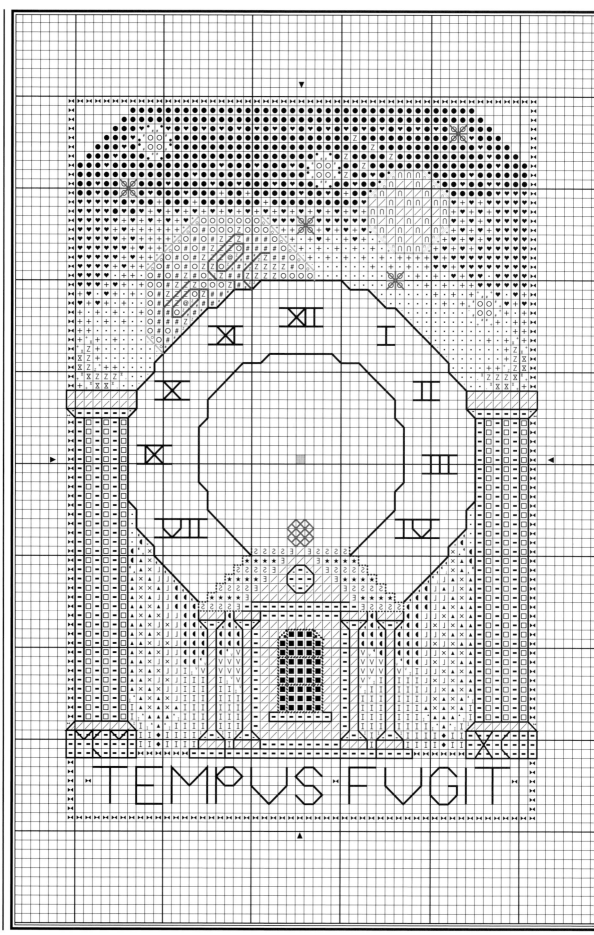

Cross stitch in two strands except for the window panes and the light grey on the pillars which are half cross stitch

DMC	Anchor	Madeira	Symbol	Colour
Ecru	387	Ecru	//	Ecru
311	148	1008	●●	Dark blue
312	979	1005	♥♥	Blue
322	978	1004	++	Medium blue
400	351	2305	◆◆	Brown
415	398	1803	nn	Grey
437	362	2012	★★	Light brown
469	267	1503	▲▲	Dark green
470	266	1502	××	Medium green
471	265	1501	⌐⌐	Green
472	253	1414	II	Light green
644	391	1907	--	Light grey
680	901	2210	@@	Dark gold
726	295	0109	ZZ	Warm yellow
727	293	0110	##	Yellow
738	361	2013	ss	Medium brown
742	303	0114	⋊⋉	Orange
775	975	1001	◀◀	Very light blue
919	340	0313	϶϶	Terracotta
3078	292	0102	oo	Light yellow
3325	144	1002	··	Light blue
3743	869	0807	vv	Warm grey
783	306	2211	▶◀	Toffee(silk)

Half Cross Stitch in two strands

DMC	Anchor	Madeira	Symbol	Colour
Ecru	387	Ecru	▫▫	Ecru
311	148	1008	■■	Dark Blue

Backstitch all lines in number of strands indicated

DMC	Anchor	Madeira	Colour
645	400	1811	Dark grey(1) pillars and facade
680	901	2210	Dark gold(1) sun face details
726	295	0109	Warm yellow(1) sun outline
919	340	0313	Terracotta(1) roof outline
Ecru	387	Ecru	Ecru(2) window
415	398	1803	Grey(1) moon outline
783	306	2211	Toffee(silk) clock face(1), numerals and letters(2)
Glissengloss no 03			Metallic gold(1) details

Finished size: Stitch count 79 high x 53 wide

Fabric and approximate finished design area:

11 aida 7⅛x4⅞in

14 aida 5⅝x3¾in

18 aida 4¼x3in

For Tempus Fugit
You will need

❀ 14HPI damask aida - 11x9in (28x23cm), cream

❀ Stranded cotton - as listed in the key

❀ Tapestry needle - size 24

❀ Mantel clock

Sending in the Clowns

Why not indulge in some clowning around with our colourful tumbling troop?

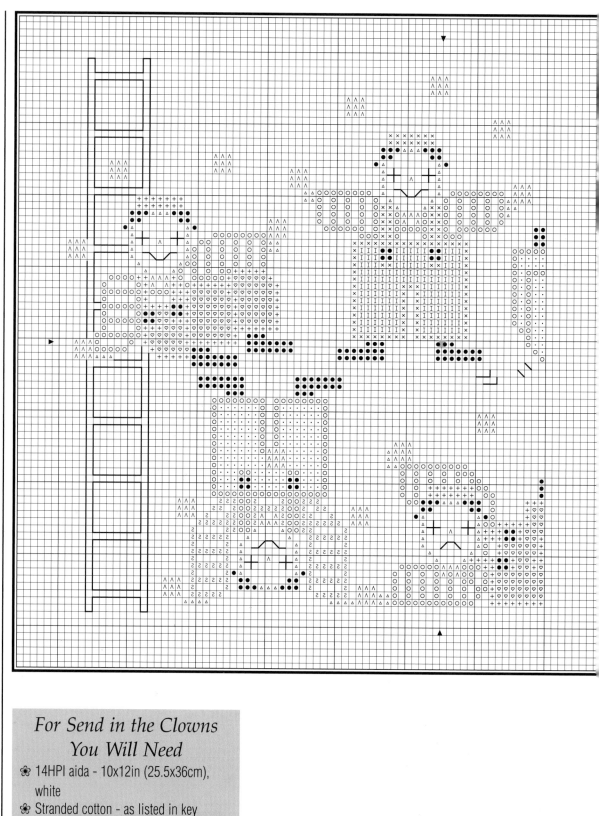

For Send in the Clowns You Will Need

- ❀ 14HPI aida - 10x12in (25.5x36cm), white
- ❀ Stranded cotton - as listed in key
- ❀ Tapestry needle - size 24
- ❀ Red frame - 9½x11¾in (24.5x29.8cm)
- ❀ Mounts - yellow and red, with 6¼x8¼in (16.1x21cm) opening

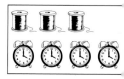

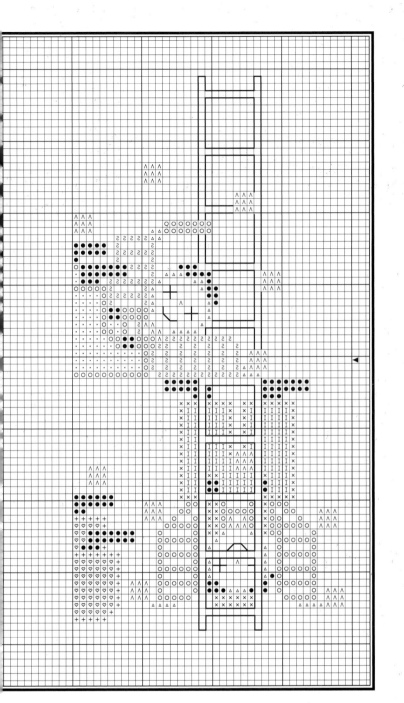

Working Instructions

Work the cross stitch in two strands of cotton

The back stitch on the ladder and faces is worked in one strand of black

You can also stitch the clowns individually to make up small pictures or cards.

Send in the Clowns Key

Anchor	DMC	Madeira		Colour
Cross stitch in two strands				
098	553	0712	2 2	Purple
136	800	0910	· ·	Light blue
139	797	0912	o o	Blue
203	564	1211	♡ ♡	Light green
205	912	1213	+ +	Green
301	744	0110	I I	Light yellow
302	743	0114	× ×	Yellow
335	606	0209	∧ ∧	Scarlet
403	310	Black	● ●	Black
868	758	0403	▵ ▵	Flesh pink

Anchor	DMC	Madeira		Colour
Backstitch all lines in one strand				
403	310	Black		Black ladders, clown details

Finished size: Stitch count 77 high x 106 wide
Fabric and approximate finished design area:
11 aida 7x9⅝ in
14 aida 5½x7½ in
18 aida 4⅛x5¾ in

Plain Sailing

❀ ❀ ❀

Set off on a voyage of discovery with our
colourful nautical designs.

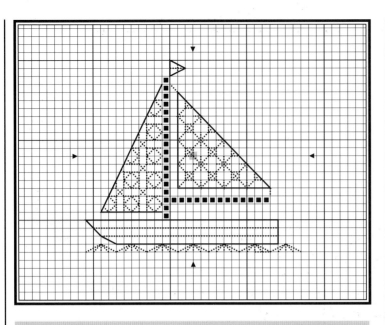

Blackwork Boat Key

DMC	Anchor	Madeira		Colour
Cross stitch in three strands				
310	403	Black	■■	Black
Backstitch all lines in one strand				
310	403	Black		Black
Backstitch all lines in three strands				
310	403	Black	⌐	Black ship outlines

Our model was stitched using DMC threads; the Anchor and Madeira conversions are not necessarily exact colour equivalents.

Finished size: Stitch count 24 high x 28 wide
Fabric and approximate finished design area:
11HPI aida 2 ⅛ in x 2 ⅜ in 14HPI aida 1 ¾ in x 2 in 18HPI aida 1 ⅜ in x 1 ¼ in

For Blackwork Boat You will need

- ❀ 14HPI aida - 5½x4½in (13.75x11.25cm), white
- ❀ Stranded cotton - as listed in the key
- ❀ Tapestry needle - size 24
- ❀ flexi-hoop - 4x3in (10x7.5cm), wood effect

For Sailing Boat You will need

- ❀ 14HPI aida - 5x5in (12.5x12.5cm), blue
- ❀ Stranded cotton - as listed in the key
- ❀ Tapestry needle -size 24
- ❀ Flexi-hoop - 3½in (8,75cm) round, blue rope effect

Sailing Boat Key

DMC	Anchor	Madeira		Colour
Cross stitch in two strands				
White	001	White	· ·	White
666	046	0210	o o	Red
912	205	1213	× ×	Green
Cross stitch in two strands blending one strand of each colour				
310	403	Black	● ●	Black
645	400	1809		Grey

Our model was stitched using DMC threads; the Anchor and Madeira conversions are not necessarily exact colour equivalents.

Finished size: Stitch count 27 high x 31 wide
Fabric and approximate finished design area:
11HPI aida 2 ½ in x 2 ⅞ in 14HPI aida 2 in x 2 ¼ in 18HPI aida 1 ½ in x 1 ¾ in

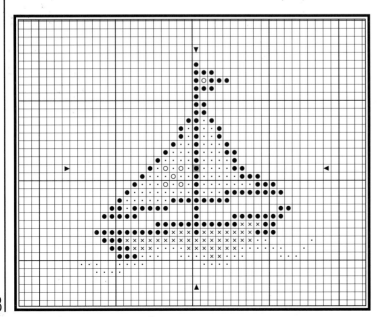

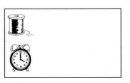

Working Instructions

All the projects are worked in two strands of stranded cotton, with one strand for the back stitch. Follow the instructions on pp. 15-17 for making up the projects into cards and fitting into small frames.

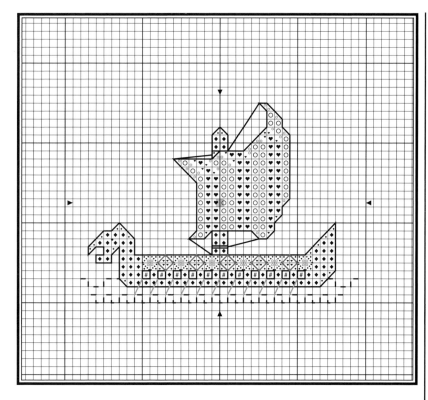

For Viking Ship You will need

❊ 14HPI aida - 6x6in (15x15cm), white
❊ Stranded cotton - as listed in the key
❊ Tapestry needle - size 24
❊ Frame - 4¼x4¼in (10.6x10.6cm), red wood
½oz wadding - 3¼x3¼in (8.2x8.2cm)

Viking Ship Key

Anchor	DMC	Madeira		Colour
Cross stitch in two strands				
46	666	0210	♥♥	Red
36	413	1713	# #	Dark grey
58	433	2008	♦♦	Dark brown
26	Ecru	Ecru	○○	Ecru
Backstitch all lines in one strand				
36	413	1713		Dark grey ropes and outline of ship
Backstitch all lines in two strands				
46	666	0210		Red Outline of shields
69	517	1108		Dark blue waves
75	420	2105		Medium brown oars

Anchor	DMC	Madeira		Colour
926	Ecru	Ecru		Ecru outline of shields
French knot in one strand				
046	666	0210	••	Red eye on head

Our model was stitched using Anchor threads; the DMC and Madeira conversions are not necessarily exact colour equivalents.

Finished size: Stitch count 25 high x 36 wide
Fabric and approximate finished design area:
11HPI aida 2 ¼ in x 3 ¼ in 14HPI aida 1 ¾ in x 2 ½ in
18HPI aida 1 ⅜ in x 2 in

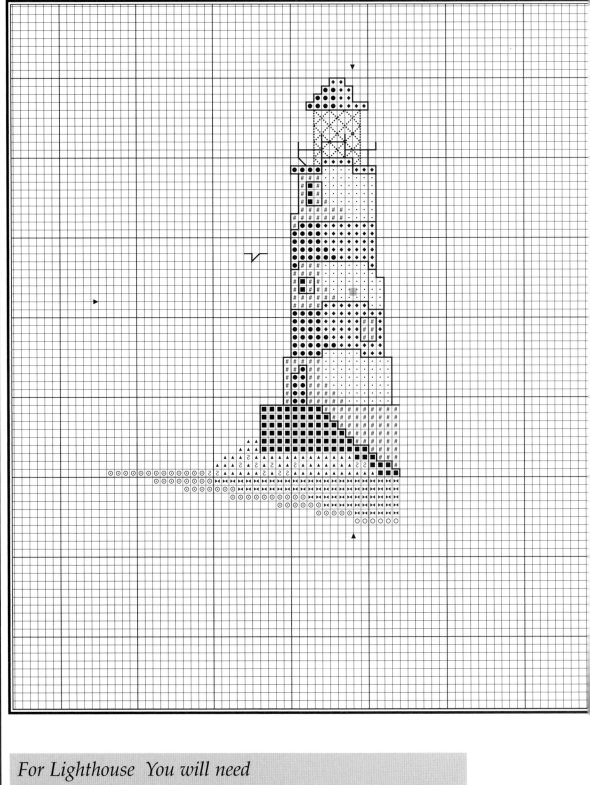

For Lighthouse You will need

❀ 14HPI aida - 10½x10½in (26.3x26.3cm), light blue

❀ Stranded cotton - as listed in the key

❀ Tapestry needle - size 24

❀ Frame - 8½x8½in (21.3x21.3cm), grey-blue with gilt edge

❀ Mounts - two, with a 4¾x4¾in (11.9x11.9cm) opening, one blue and one red

❀ 2oz wadding - 4¾x4¾in (11.9x11.9cm)

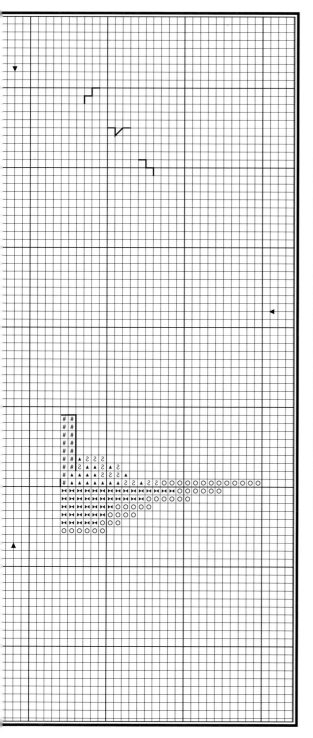

Lighthouse Key

DMC	Anchor	Madeira		Colour
Cross stitch in two strands				
White	002	White	· ·	White
318	399	1801	# #	Grey
321	013	0510	◆ ◆	Red
612	832	2108	ƨ ƨ	Sand
816	044	0512	● ●	Dark red
829	906	2113	▲ ▲	Olive
926	850	1707	⊙ ⊙	Medium turquoise
927	849	1708	○ ○	Light turquoise
3768	840	1706	⋈ ⋈	Turquoise
3799	779	1713	■ ■	Dark grey

Backstitch all lines in one strand				
413	401	1714		Slate grey lighthouse outline
816	044	0512		Dark red lighthouse detail

Our model was stitched using DMC threads; the Anchor and Madeira conversions are not necessarily exact colour equivalents.

Finished size: Stitch count 56 high x 64 wide
Fabric and approximate finished design area:
11HPI aida 5 in x 5 ⅞ in
14HPI aida 4 in x 4 ½ in
18HPI aida 3 ⅛ in x 3 ½ in

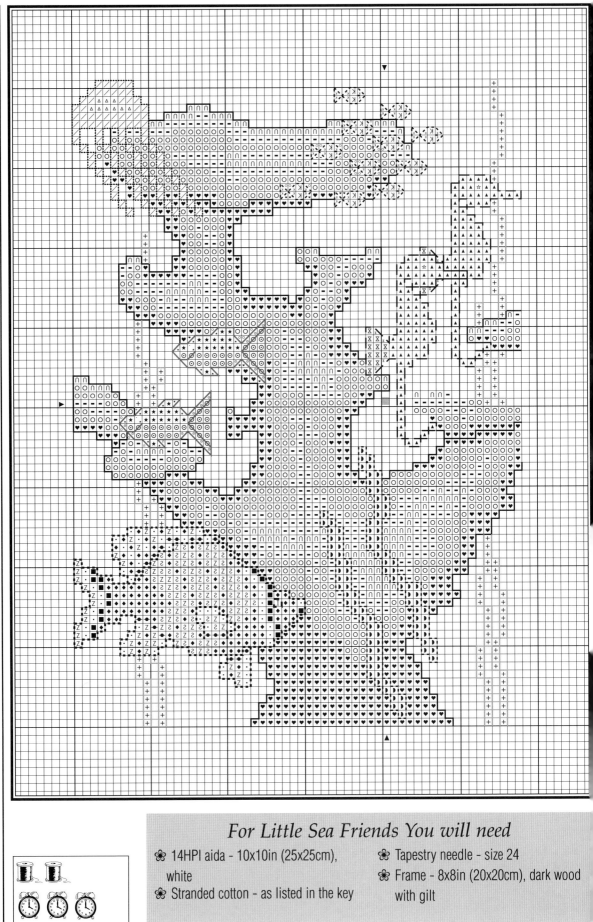

For Little Sea Friends You will need

❊ 14HPI aida - 10x10in (25x25cm), white

❊ Stranded cotton - as listed in the key

❊ Tapestry needle - size 24

❊ Frame - 8x8in (20x20cm), dark wood with gilt

Little Sea Friends Key

DMC	Anchor	Madeira		Colour
Cross stitch in two strands				
307	289	0104	· ·	Light yellow
310	403	Black	■ ■	Black
334	145	1004	▵ ▵	Blue
349	013	0212	♥ ♥	Dark salmon
351	011	0214	○ ○	Apricot
352	010	0406	– –	Medium salmon
353	008	0304	∩ ∩	Light salmon
501	218	1205	◆ ◆	Dark green
550	102	0714	♦ ♦	Dark violet
552	100	0713	ƨ ƨ	Medium violet
554	097	0711	z z	Pinky violet
600	065	0704	▯ ▯	Dark rose pink
742	303	0114	κ κ	Medium orange
744	301	0110	v v	Yellow
871	304	0203	× ×	Orange
909	923	1303	★ ★	Medium green
913	209	1212	○ ○	Light green
924	851	1706	☆ ☆	Dark blue green
958	187	1114	I I	Turquoise
3013	843	1605	x̄ x̄	Sandy green
3325	129	0910	⁄ ⁄	Light blue
3347	266	1408	+ +	Bright green
Cross stitch in two strands blending one strand of each colour				
420	375	2105	▲ ▲	Dark fawn
3013	843	1605		Sandy green
891	029	0411	≲ ≲	Pink
3706	033	0409		Dark pink
Cross stitch in three strands blending one strand of each colour				
501	218	1205		Dark green
552	112	0713	▸ ▸	Lavender
958	187	1114		Turquoise
Backstitch all lines in one strand				
334	145	1004		Blue outline of jellyfish
420	375	2105		Dark fawn seahorses
501	218	1205		Dark green coral tree
550	102	0714		Dark violet large fish
703	238	1307		Leaf green seaweed
913	209	1212		Light green starfish and seaflower
924	851	1706		Dark blue green goldfish
909	923	1303		Medium green pair of green fish
958	187	1114		Turquoise punk fish
French Knots				
307	289	0104	· ·	Light Yellow eel's eyes

Our model was stitched using DMC threads; the Anchor and Madeira conversions are not necessarily exact colour equivalents.

Finished size: Stitch count 81 high x 81 wide
Fabric and approximate finished design area:
11HPI aida 7 ⅜ in x 7 ⅜ in 14HPI aida 5 ¾ in x 5 ¾ in
18HPI aida 4 ½ in x 4 ½ in

Earth laughs in flowers

EMERSON

Ralph Waldo Emerson
1803–1882

Emerson was the most celebrated American
and nearly as famous in England,
essayist and Unitarian minister
among his many talents was the
genius of Wit and wisdom
Emerson's

Earth Laughs in Flowers

An intricate design recreating the delicate watercolour effect of fresh country flowers.

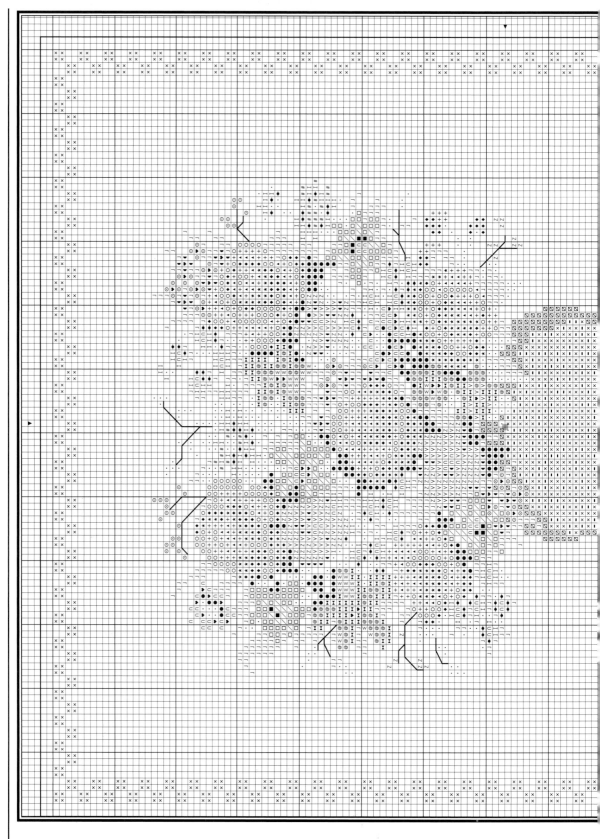

Working Instructions

This flower sampler is worked in a single strand of stranded cotton on the finer fabric to give it a beautifully detailed look.

Work the cross stitch in one strand of stranded cotton

The back stitch is worked in one strand of antique blue for the border

and lettering, and one strand of pine green for the flower stems.

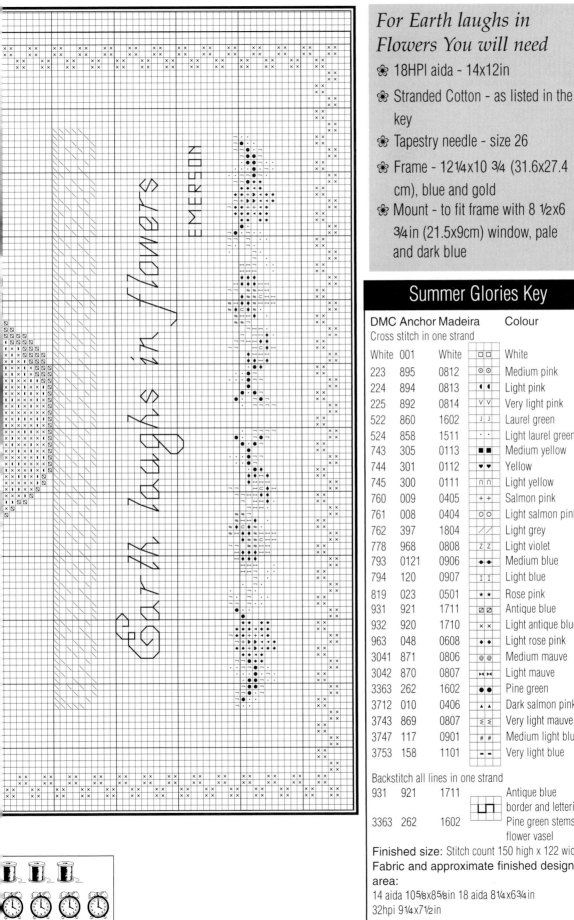

EMERSON

Earth laughs in flowers

For Earth laughs in Flowers You will need

- ❀ 18HPI aida - 14x12in
- ❀ Stranded Cotton - as listed in the key
- ❀ Tapestry needle - size 26
- ❀ Frame - 12¼x10 ¾ (31.6x27.4 cm), blue and gold
- ❀ Mount - to fit frame with 8 ½x6 ¾in (21.5x9cm) window, pale and dark blue

Summer Glories Key

DMC	Anchor	Madeira		Colour
Cross stitch in one strand				
White	001	White	□□	White
223	895	0812	⊙⊙	Medium pink
224	894	0813	◖◖	Light pink
225	892	0814	ᴠᴠ	Very light pink
522	860	1602	⌐⌐	Laurel green
524	858	1511	··	Light laurel green
743	305	0113	■■	Medium yellow
744	301	0112	♥♥	Yellow
745	300	0111	∩∩	Light yellow
760	009	0405	++	Salmon pink
761	008	0404	○○	Light salmon pink
762	397	1804	⁄⁄	Light grey
778	968	0808	ᴢᴢ	Light violet
793	0121	0906	◆◆	Medium blue
794	120	0907	ɪɪ	Light blue
819	023	0501	★★	Rose pink
931	921	1711	⊘⊘	Antique blue
932	920	1710	××	Light antique blue
963	048	0608	◆◆	Light rose pink
3041	871	0806	@@	Medium mauve
3042	870	0807	⋈⋈	Light mauve
3363	262	1602	●●	Pine green
3712	010	0406	▲▲	Dark salmon pink
3743	869	0807	≲≲	Very light mauve
3747	117	0901	##	Medium light blue
3753	158	1101	--	Very light blue

Backstitch all lines in one strand				
931	921	1711		Antique blue border and lettering
3363	262	1602		Pine green stems in flower vasel

Finished size: Stitch count 150 high x 122 wide
Fabric and approximate finished design area:
14 aida 10⅝x8⅝in 18 aida 8¼x6¾in
32hpi 9¼x7½in

The Flowering of Passions

A delightful selection of country flower motifs incorporating some unusual finishing ideas.

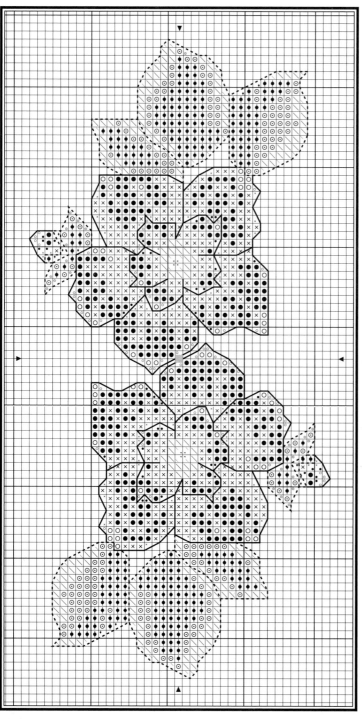

Les Fleurs Key

DMC	Anchor	Madeira		Colour
Cross stitch in two strands				
608	333	0205	× ×	Dark orange
703	239	1306	╱╱	Light green
726	295	0109	▲ ▲	Light yellow
890	683	1314	◆ ◆	Dark green
971	316	0203	● ●	Orange
972	298	0107	○ ○	Yellow
987	244	1403	◎ ◎	Medium green

Backstitch all lines in one strand				
349	013	0212		Dark peach Flower outline
890	683	1314		Deep green Leaves outline

Our model was stitched using DMC threads; the Anchor and Madeira conversions are not necessarily exact colour equivalents.

Finished size: Stitch count 39 high x 80 wide
Fabric and approximate finished design area:
11HPI aida 3⅝x7⅜in 14HPI aida 3x5¾in
18HPI aida 2¼x4½in

For Les Fleurs
You will need

❀ 18HPI aida - 3¾in (9.4cm) wide, length and colour to suit your towel
❀ Stranded cotton - as listed in the key
❀ Tapestry needle - size 26
❀ Sewing kit
❀ Towel

To Make Up the Towel

Cut a piece of aida 3¾in (9.5cm) wide and long enough to fit across the width of your towel.

Work the design in the centre of the aida using one strand for the cross stitch and for the back stitch.

Turn under the edges along the length of your aida, leaving five holes on either side of the flower. Pin to the end of your towel, 1½in (3.8cm) from the bottom and lined up with the sides.

Sew the aida on to the towel with small invisible stitches.

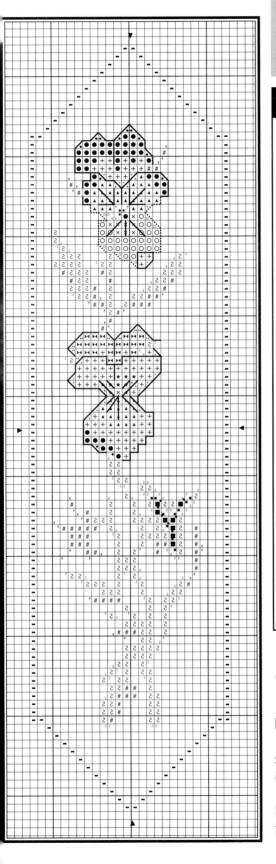

For Wild Pansy Bookmark
You will need

❀ 1HPI aida - 7½x2½in (18.8x6.3cm), white

❀ Stranded cotton - as listed in the key

❀ White cotton - for finishing the bookmark

❀ Tapestry needle - size 26

Wild Pansy Bookmark Key

DMC	Anchor	Madeira		Colour
Cross stitch in two strands				
White	001	White	★ ★	White
310	403	Black	– –	Black
520	862	1514	# #	Dark green
550	102	0714	+ +	Purple
553	098	0713	● ●	Medium violet
727	293	0110	▲ ▲	Light yellow
741	314	0201	× ×	Orange
917	089	0706	◄ ►	Dark cerise
973	290	0105	○ ○	Yellow
3347	266	1408	ϱ ϱ	Medium green
3776	326	0310	■ ■	Gold

Backstitch all lines in one strand

550	102	0714	Purple
973	290	0105	Yellow

French knots in one strand

550	102	0714	Purple

Our model was stitched using DMC threads; the Anchor and Madeira conversions are not necessarily exact colour equivalents.

Finished size: Stitch count 96 high x 26 wide
Fabric and approximate finished design area:
11HPI aida 8¼x2⅜in 14HPI aida 6⅞x1⅞in
18HPI aida 5⅜x1½in

To Make Up the Bookmark

Turn under ⅜in (1cm) along the long edges of each bookmark. With white thread stitch the seams in place.

Continue stitching, following the shape of the black cross stitches through a single layer of aida. Repeat this at the opposite end of the bookmark.

Carefully snip the horizontal threads one square from the backstitch and remove them at each end of the bookmark. Trim the fringe into a curve.

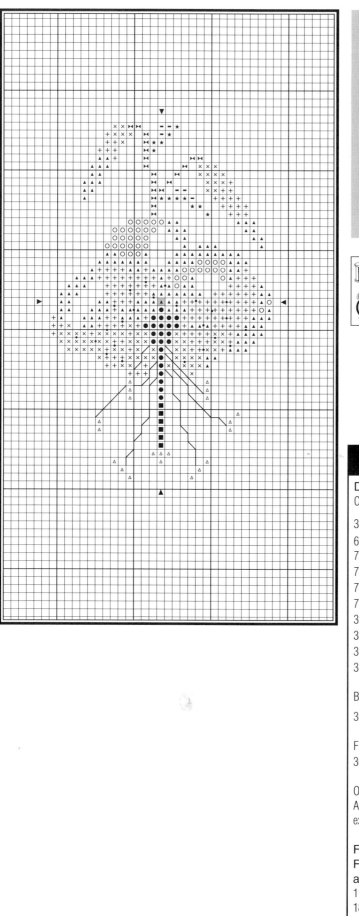

For Tiger Lily You will need

❀ 27HPI AIDA - 6x4¼ in (15x10.6cm), cream
❀ Stranded cotton - as listed in the key
❀ Tapestry needle - size 26
❀ Card - 4x3in (10x7.5cm) with an oval opening, cream
❀ 2oz wadding - 4x3in (10.7.5cm), oval

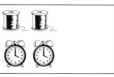

Tiger Lily Key

DMC	Anchor	Madeira		Colour
Cross stitch in two strands				
300	352	2304	▵ ▵	Brown
613	956	2109	● ●	Taupe
721	324	0309	× ×	Dark orange
741	314	0201	+ +	Orange
742	303	0114	▲ ▲	Light orange
743	305	0113	○ ○	Yellow
3047	886	2205	■ ■	Sandstone
3345	268	1406	★ ★	Dark green
3346	257	1504	− −	Medium green
3371	382	2004	⋈ ⋈	Dark brown

Backstitch all lines in two strands

3047	886	2205	Sandstone

French knots in one strand

300	352	2304	• •	Brown

Our model was stitched using DMC threads; the Anchor and Madeira conversions are not necessarily exact colour equivalents.

Finished size: Stitch count 45 high x 29 wide
Fabric and approximate finished design area:
11HPI aida 4⅛x2¾ in 14HPI aida 3¼x2⅛ in
18HPI aida 2½x1⅝ in

Dog Rose Bookmark Key

DMC	Anchor	Madeira		Colour
Cross stitch in two strands				
307	289	0104	◆ ◆	Yellow
310	403	Black	– –	Black
520	862	1514	# #	Dark green
603	057	0714	⊙ ⊙	Dark pink
776	024	0503	▲ ▲	Medium pink
819	271	0502	+ +	Light pink
3347	266	1408	× ×	Medium green

Backstitch all lines in one strand				
603	057	0714	⌐⌐	Dark pink

French knots in one strand				
307	289	0104	• •	Yellow

Our model was stitched using DMC threads; the Anchopr and Madeira conversions are not necessarily exact colour equivalents.

Finished size: Stitch count 96 high x 26 wide
Fabric and approximate finished design area:
11HPI aida 8¼x2⅜in 14HPI aida 6⅞x1⅞in
18HPI aida 5⅜x1½in

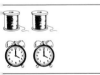

For Dog Rose Bookmark You will need

❀ 18HPI aida - 7½x2½in (18.8x6.3cm), white
❀ Stranded cotton - as listed in the key
❀ White cotton - for finishing the bookmark
❀ Tapestry needle - size 26

To make up the bookmark, follow the instructions for Wild Pansy on p.121.

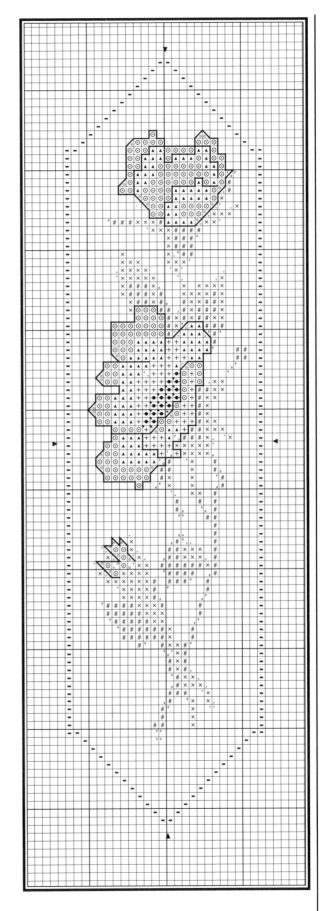

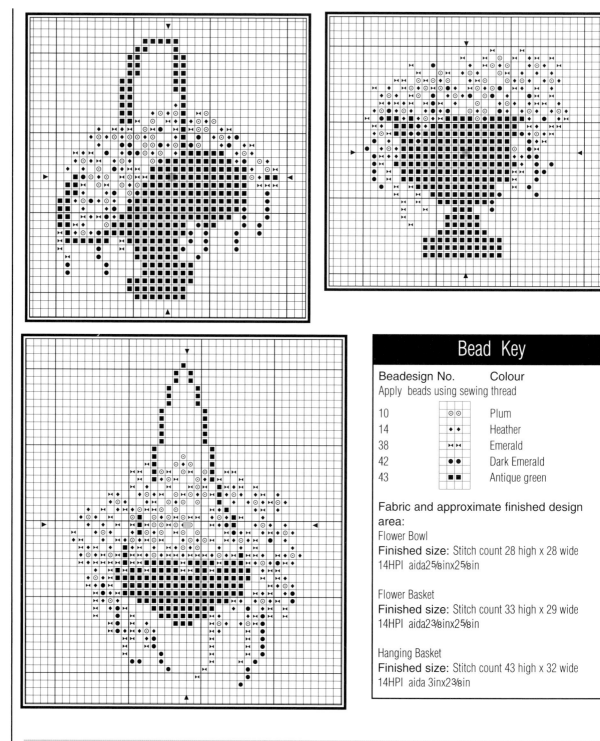

Bead Key

Beadesign No.   **Colour**

Apply beads using sewing thread

No.		Colour
10	⊙ ⊙	Plum
14	◆ ◆	Heather
38	⋈ ⋈	Emerald
42	● ●	Dark Emerald
43	■ ■	Antique green

Fabric and approximate finished design area:

Flower Bowl
Finished size: Stitch count 28 high x 28 wide
14HPI aida 2⅝in x 2⅝in

Flower Basket
Finished size: Stitch count 33 high x 29 wide
14HPI aida 2⅜in x 2⅝in

Hanging Basket
Finished size: Stitch count 43 high x 32 wide
14HPI aida 3in x 2⅜in

For Beads You will need

❋ 14HPI aida - 6x6in (15x15cm), ivory

❋ Polyester sewing thread - ivory

❋ Needle - sharp size 10

❋ Seed beads - Rocailles size 11/0: Antique green (Beadesign 43):- 170 for the hanging basket; 220 for the flowering urn; 265 for the flower basket. Emerald green (Beadesign 38):- 110 for the hanging basket; 65 for the flowering urn; 35 for the flower basket. Dark emerald (Beadesign 42):- 50 for the hanging basket; 45 for the flowering urn; 60 or the flower basket. Heather (Beadesign 14):- 115 for the hanging basket; 70 for the flowering urn; 60 for the flower basket. Plum (Beadesign 10):- 65 for the hanging basket; 40 for the flowering urn; 45 for the flower basket.

Flexi-hoop - 4x4in (10x10cm), sage green

Working with Beads

Each colour is represented by a different symbol. Follow the chart and key for the placement of each bead.

The beads are attached with a half cross stitch using sewing thread and a sharp needle. Bring your needle up at the bottom left of each square and pick up the bead on to the needle before pushing the needle back into the top right of the square.

If you want to move from one area to another while stitching, you should move no more than four stitches at a time. If you need to move across a larger area, you should catch the thread on to the back of your work or the tension of the beads will become slack.

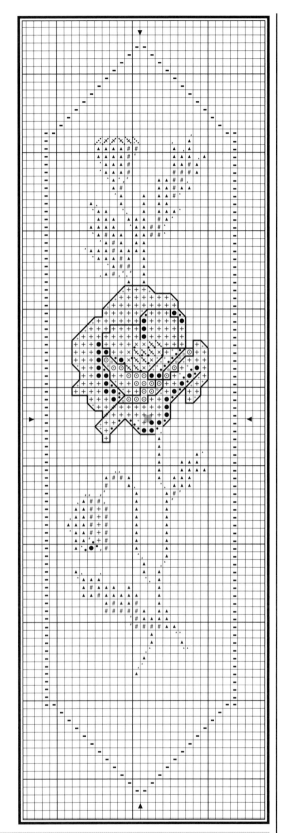

Poppy Bookmark Key

DMC	Anchor	Madeira		Colour
Cross stitch in two strands				
310	403	Black	− −	Black
520	862	1514	# #	Dark green
725	306	0113	× ×	Yellow
760	009	0405	⊙ ⊙	Pink
815	022	0513	● ●	Dark red
817	019	0212	+ +	Red
3347	266	1408	▲ ▲	Medium green

Backstitch all lines in one strand

| 815 | 022 | 0513 | ⌐⌐ | Dark red outline poppy |
| 310 | 403 | Black | | Black stamens |

French knots in one strand

| 310 | 403 | Black | • • | Black flower detail |

Our model was stitched using DMC threads; the Anchor and Madeira conversions are not necessarily exact colour equivalents.

Finished size: Stitch count 96 high x 26 wide
Fabric and approximate finished design area:
11HPI aida 8¼x2⅜in   14HPI aida 6⅞x1⅞in
18HPI aida 5⅜x1½in

For Poppy Bookmark You will need

❀ 18HPI aida - 7½x2½in (18.8x6.3cm), white
❀ Stranded cotton - as listed in the key
❀ White cotton - for finishing the bookmark
❀ Tapestry needle - size 26

To make up the bookmark, follow the instructions for Wild Pansy Bookmark on p. 121.

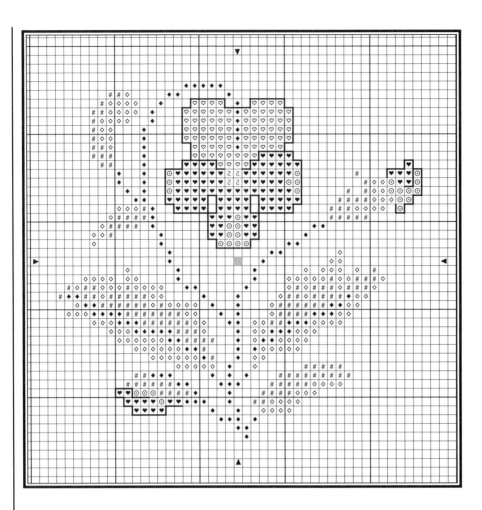

Lavender Bag Key

DMC	Anchor	Madeira			Colour
Cross stitch in two strands					
211	342	0801	♡	♡	Mauve
3041	873	0806	♥	♥	Med dusky mauve
3042	869	0807	⊙	⊙	Light dusky mauve
3078	292	0102	ƨ	ƨ	Yellow
3348	265	1209	◇	◇	Light green
3362	862	1514	◆	◆	Dark green
3363	861	1602	#	#	Medium green

Backstitch all lines in one strand

3362	862	1514		Dark green

Our model was stitched using DMC threads; the Anchor and Madeira conversions are not necessarily exact colour equivalents.

Finished size: Stitch count 41 high x 43 wide
Fabric and approximate finished design area:
11HPI aida 3 ¾ in x 3 ⅞ in
14HPI aida 2 ⅞ in x 3 in
18HPI aida 2 ¼ in x 2 ⅜ in

For Lavender Bag You will need

- ❀ 14HPI aida - 5½x4½in (13.8x10.6cm), white
- ❀ Stranded cotton - as listed in the key
- ❀ Tapestry needle - size 24
- ❀ Cotton lace - 9in (22.5cm) of ½in (1.3cm) wide, white
- ❀ Ribbon - 20in (50cm) of ¼ in (6mm) wide, mauve
- ❀ Backing fabric - 5½x4¼in (13.8x10.6cm), white satin
- ❀ Sewing kit - needle, thread, pins etc
- ❀ Ribbon rose - mauve

To Make Up the Lavender Bag

Work the design starting 2¼in (5.7cm) from the top of the large flower.

When you have completed the design, place the aida and the backing fabric right sides together and, with a ¼in (6mm) seam allowance, stitch along three sides leaving the top open.

Turn the bag to the right side out. Turn over the top ¼in (6mm) of the bag and sew in place.

Sew the lace around the top edge of the bag. Sew the ribbon rose ½in (1.3cm) from the top. You can now fill the bag up with pot pourri and tie the top with a piece of matching ribbon.